Jimmie & Ginney,

What an honor serving Jesus with you. I'm always encouraged when I see ya'll!

Who Will Cross the Jordan?

Love Doug Stringer

by Doug Stringer

GRATEFUL ACKNOWLEDGEMENTS

Many thanks to my dear friend Gregory N. Carmona for all the transcribing and valuable editorial assistance, but especially for believing in me and inspiring me to get the message out.

My appreciation to Susie Wolf for the many late night hours at the office transcribing, typing and re-typing, editing and re-editing, and to Joann Cole Webster for her helpful insights and constructive criticism.

Thanks to my many friends, staff and co-laborers who have stood with me through not only the victories, but through my failures as well, and who are still learning to walk out the message of this book with me.

Lastly, I would like to warmly acknowledge my CIRCLE of dedicated ministry friends who are earnestly seeking to be consecrated and to be more like Him daily!

DEDICATION

This book is dedicated to all of those who are weary . . . to all of those who are earnestly searching for the "Promised Land"—even that perfect rest of faith which is in Christ Jesus . . .

TABLE OF CONTENTS

Foreword

In the context of life and the annals of individual history, there are circumstances, events and friendships that mark milestones along each way. Circumstances and events leave their impact for good or bad, cause change in direction and character, and are unforgettable. People make impressions that are indelible, inspire and motivate, or demean and diminish ones own desires and ambitions.

When such people come along whose example others are encouraged to emulate, to attempt to do greater things than ever dreamed or imagined, that person is a leader. Some persons simply happen to influence; leaders determine to influence.

When Doug Stringer first made his appearance in my life and in our ministry, seeking to accomplish something never tried before and believing he could do it, I realized here was an unusual man—but I regarded time as the real proof of his ability.

Time, like light, makes things manifest.

Given enough time, the real character of a man will become known through his thoughts, words, and actions. Time proves men. "Fame can come in a moment, but greatness comes with longevity."

Time proved Doug to me personally. Not only did he accomplish that which he set out to do with our ministry, but he achieved greater things than imagined as his vision grew and his ministry multiplied.

Today, on more than one continent, there are others who have been inspired by Doug to achieve great things for God. Young men and women alike have been challenged, inspired, and encouraged to develop Godly character and, in obedience to Christ's Great Commission, to go into all the world and make disciples.

Doug's world has not been the couth, cultured, high-gloss realm of the rich and famous, but the debased, diseased, defamed and disallowed. Substance and sexually abused, sick and shamed, reviled and rejected men and women have found acceptance; forgiveness; moral, physical and spiritual healing and health; and returned to a normal life free from dependencies and addictions.

To rescue the perishing, Doug has needed to challenge the righteous, to inspire them to works of the Good Samaritan who did not ignore the needy, but gave of *himself to see to their help* and health.

Doug Stringer is an unsung hero to many in the world today, but there are those who sing his praises for the remarkable and miraculous change in their lives, saving them from hell both spiritually and literally through the message of grace, hope, love and life in Jesus Christ. He has become a friend who determined to influence and left his mark in their lives.

In the passage of time, he has learned the principles of God's Kingdom, applied and practiced them to success both personally and ministerially. From his life comes truth learned in the crucible of experience. Just one great truth can change a society, a world, a person. Just one truth from Doug's book can change your life.

This book can be your best friend, just as Doug is to so many.

Like them, I am proud to have Doug as my friend.

Edwin Louis Cole

1.

WHY CROSS THE JORDAN

The title of this book was the theme of our fifth annual Spiritual Impact/Evangelism Conference in Houston in 1990. Leading up to the Conference I had been seeking the Lord for His heart for those who would attend, as well as for all His people. I felt the need to hear from God more keenly than I ever had.

For years I had been pounding the sidewalks of Houston in the early morning hours, reaching out to the young, the lost, the street people. A band of Christians had joined me in "Jericho Marches" around satanic rock concerts and in "Jericho Drives" around our city to pull down spiritual strongholds. We had led witnessing teams during Mardis Gras', Beach Blitz' during school breaks, and had conducted massive soul-winning campaigns, Christian concerts, street feeds, and every kind of Christian rally imaginable. By my early twenties, I felt I had seen it all. The tragedies of the streets and of our youth culture are so real. Young people who are prostitutes, drug addicts, bums, homosexuals, topless dancers, runaways—unaware of how they got where they are, unsure of what they are doing, hopelessly feeling they are being used as pawns by a force beyond their control.

The Evangelism Conference we started in Houston is mainly for those who have a burden for the lost, but who also have a longing in their souls to draw closer to Jesus. We attract men and women who are ministering around the world on street corners and in back alleys in the ugliest spots on earth, to society's refuse living there. Willing to remain anonymous, these are "front line soldiers" in God's army. Their works go unnoticed by millions, but mean much to the outcast people they reach.

I have worked side by side with many of them, and call them brothers and sisters, but to see the spiritual wealth of their lives at one time, in one conference is powerful. Each year my amazement has grown, and on the eve of this fifth conference, I was overwhelmed. The courage, stamina, persistence, and sheer faith of these warriors made me shrink in disgust at the smallness I often felt in my own spirit and in my ministry. Now I was to address them. I was to give them a message that would bring rest to their weary hearts, encourage them, boost their faith, enlarge their vision. Something they could hang on to. For many of them a message to last a year before they would be ministered to like that again.

WEARY TRAVELERS

As I prayed, I came to realize that we are all at times weary travelers. As we journey through our Christian lives, both the minister and layman, we become weary. We desire to be used of God, to have His anointing flow freely through us during every hour of the day. But we grow tired, weary of the fight, depleted by the energy the ministry requires. I began to picture Jesus Christ as an oasis of life for God's people. A watering hole in a parched land. I thought of the Israelites strug-gling in the wilderness between Egypt and Canaan. God's perfect plan for us is not simply to deliver us from the world (Egypt), but to deliver us into a place of victory and rest (The Promised Land). When we lose sight of our ultimate "rest" in Jesus we can dry up and die in a wilderness. Even when on the outside we continue pressing on, we can die inside. We lose the expression of His Person, His Power, and His Anointing in and through our lives.

As I meditated on this, God began to show me how much He desired intimacy with His people. He desires to lead people out of a spiritual Egypt and into a Land of Promise, going by way of wilderness trials. In order to get there, in order to make it, we have to cross the Jordan.

In the book of Numbers, a whole generation of Israelites died in a wilderness of unbelief. Another two and a half tribes refused to cross the Jordan and settled right where they were. So close to their "Promised Land," and yet unwilling to continue further. Many Christians today have become so weary in their walk through the wilder-ness that they stand at the banks of the Jordan and say, "Lord, I've been traveling so long. Can't I just stay on this side of the Jordan?" They said in essence, "This land looks good enough. I'm too tired to fight giants in Canaan for my inheritance. I'll just settle right here."

ENTERING THE PROMISED LAND

Just because people are Christians doesn't

mean they have crossed the Jordan and entered the "Promised Land". Many never do. There are prerequisites to crossing the Jordan. There are very important issues we must deal with before we can enter. The question is, "Do we have the courage to deal with those issues so we can cross and enter the Promised Land?"

In the Word, we see that immediately preceding the return of Jesus, judgment will begin at the House of God (1 Pet.4:17). Jesus, (the Bridegroom) is coming back for a Church (the bride) that is without spot or blemish (Eph. 5:27). Therefore, judgment is coming to prepare the heart of the Bride for the Bridegroom.

The judgment fire of God can be a refining fire that makes us shine as pure gold, or it can be a consuming fire that destroys us for all eternity. It may depend on the spiritual clothes we're wearing. Shadrach, Meshach and Abednego were thrown into a fiery furnace, but came out without even the smell of smoke on their clothes (Dan. 3:27). If they had been clothed in the "world's" garments, they would have been consumed in fire in the same way the world will be consumed by the fire of God's wrath. Instead, they wore the uncompromising garments of a consecrated heart, committed to the Lord.

The church today has a choice—either wear the garments of the world or the garments of Jesus Christ. Wearing the garments of the Lord means to hate sin and love the Lord with all our heart, soul, and might. To love God in this way is to open ourselves to truth and correction. If we are not willing to receive truth, correction and chastisement then we will not enter into the Land of Promise.

We are in great need of truth and correction today. A recent survey estimated that eighty percent of Americans considered themselves to be "born again." But, in the same survey, only thirteen percent said they would suffer persecution for the Gospel's sake. The Bible teaches that all who would live godly in Christ Jesus will suffer persecution (2 Tim. 3:12). Therefore, it would be reasonable to assume that only thirteen percent of those surveyed were truly "born again." This lackluster devotion to the Lord is a quandary for today's Church.

There are three things the Church has struggled with continually over the last 2,000 years. They are poverty, persecution and prosperity. History shows that the greatest growth and revival have come during times of poverty or persecution. During times of prosperity and material wealth Christians have tended to worship their wants instead of God. This tendency is actually a form of idolatry. The idolatry, in turn, spawns self-centeredness, complacency, apathy and compromise. Instead of fearing God, Christians tend to fear the world and what it has to offer. This has been the case in recent Church history. The chastisement of God must come to purify us if we are to reach the Promised Land.

The Lord's chastisement, like His consuming fire, can do one of two things. It will either harden our hearts and cause us to reject God's correction, which then causes Him to reject us. Or it will cause us to refocus our priorities and reevaluate our purpose for living. God chastises us to bring us back in line with truth. If we choose the pleasures of unrighteousness over the love of truth, we are in danger of deception. If we fall prey to deception, we are in danger of falling in the judgment which is to come upon all the world.

REST AND AN OUTPOURING OF THE HOLY SPIRIT

The Church today seems to be at a crossroads. If we, as individuals, are willing to come to a place of total surrender to the Father's Will,then we will be able to cross the Jordan and have rest. Included in that rest is the promised Holy Spirit, Whose anointing power we experience in our everyday lives. There is a voice calling in the wilderness today saying, "I want to pour out My Spirit on all flesh. Get your hearts ready!"

The shaking of this world will come. Prophecy confirms that. But, praise God, there is a rest that overcomes the tribulations of this world!

As He ministered to me, the Lord confirmed the theme of the conference, "Who Will Cross The Jordan?" He gave me a message for His warriors who would assemble some six to eight hundred strong. As I stood at the conference and began to preach, I felt the Spirit of the Lord course through me just as He had during those days of praying and waiting.

"Don't be discouraged! Don't be weary!" I admonished these courageous soldiers of the Lord. "Let's cross the Jordan! Let's receive truth and correction, and get ourselves in position to receive the anointing and outpouring of the Holy Spirit!"

As a result of God's Word to His troops, we did cross the Jordan during those few glorious days. The Jordan is crossable, and it is not far out of reach. There is rest and an outpouring of the Holy Spirit on the other side, if only one will cross over.

"Who will cross the Jordan?"

PART I

THE CALL TO CONSECRATION

"But as He who called you is holy, you also be holy in all your conduct, because it is written, "Be holy, for I am holy."

1 Peter 1:15-16

Therefore He says: "Awake, you who sleep, Arise from the dead, And Christ will give you light."
See then that you walk circumspectly, not as fools but as wise,
redeeming the time, because the days are evil.
Therefore do not be unwise, but understand what the will of the Lord is.
And do not be drunk with wine, in which is dissipation; but be filled with the Spirit,

Ephesians 5:14-18

2.

IT'S YOUR CHOICE

"Now therefore, fear the Lord, serve Him in sincerity and in truth, and put away the gods which your fathers served on the other side of the River and in Egypt. Serve the Lord!

And if it seems evil to you to serve the Lord, choose for yourselves this day whom you will serve, whether the gods which your fathers served that were on the other side of the River, or the gods of the Amorites, in whose land you dwell. But as for me and my house, we will serve the Lord."   **Joshua 24:14-15**

In the story of Ruth (found in the Old Testament), Naomi had two sons who married two women named Ruth and Orpah. Naomi's husband and sons died so she decided to return to Israel. Orpah chose to stay in Moab where she was from. Ruth, however, decided to go with Naomi to worship Naomi's God, the God of her husband, the true God. Ruth made a decision to follow Naomi and her Lord without any guarantees of the future. Her decision to forsake the securities and gods of Moab (a type of the world), to walk by faith and not by sight placed her in the position to become part of the lineage of Jesus.

Orpah's decision to go back to gods of the flesh sends her down in history in obscurity. We really never do hear what happens to Orpah. The decisions we make as professing Christians can place us in greatness, thus written into the lineage of Christ or send us down in history into obscurity.

Timothy, one of the Apostle Paul's converts and sons in the Lord chose to submit his heart and life to the Lord Jesus. He served Paul and the Body of Christ as unto the Lord. Another of Paul's brethren, Demas, chose to return to the world. Paul sends greetings from Demas to the Colossians. But, in 2 Tim. 4:10 Paul says, "Demas, because he loved this world, has deserted me." Demas is never heard from again in scripture. I'll go more into detail about Orpah and Demas in the chapter "Getting Egypt Out of the Heart".

Everyone has a choice to make; that choice can make the difference between an Orpah and a Ruth, or a Demas and a Timothy. Yes, *everyone* has that choice to make. Christians, we can *choose* to be a "man of faith" as did Abraham. We can *choose* to be a "man of God" as did Moses. We can choose to be that radiant "Living Sacrifice" as did the Apostle Paul. *We can choose!*

We can choose which way we want to go—the way of blessing, or the way of cursing. We can choose whom we would like to emulate—the person Judas, or the person of Jesus!

One of God's most precious gifts to man is man's own free will. Man's most precious gift to God is to *use* that free will to *choose:* to choose to love and to serve Him. No greater gift can be given back to God than for a man to freely choose to recieve His Son and to *love* the Son with all of his heart.

God will never take back this gift, nor will He

ever usurp our right to exercise it.[1] This holds true whether we choose to receive Him unto eternal life, or whether we choose to reject Him unto eternal damnation; God forbid! *He will not interfere.* He wants that decision to be solely our own. This is the way God created it to be. The Lord our God desires our *willing* love! He did not create helpless pawns, nor did He create mindless robots—mindless slaves. God, in fact, forces Himself upon *no one*, for He takes no joy in such arbitrary displays of power. Indeed, what joy would *any* father have in such a relationship? What joy is there in *forced* love? None whatsoever, for any *loving* father, that is!

As a loving Father, God does not force Himself on us. In His perfect love, God created thinking, feeling human beings which are *independent* in nature. Beings which are totally unique in creation because they have the power to *choose,* the power to *return* that freely given love. Human beings, or Humanoids as I like to call us, have the power to submit their own *independent* nature to perfect *dependence* upon God. God will never interfere with this choice, and Satan *cannot* interfere, unless we give him that right. As an earthly father rejoices in the love of his children, and their steps toward him, so does the Heavenly Father rejoice in all those who come to Him of their own free will. God rejoices in nothing other than our willing and genuine love towards Him through our free choice to obey.

I am writing about a choice that we have to make—a *choice* that we all *need* to make! It is a decision which lies with each and every individual and no one can make that decision for us.

This "choice" of course, is to choose to submit

our heart and our lives to the Lord Jesus Christ.
However, seeing that there *yet* remains a "rest" for
God's people, there is another choice which awaits
the Christian.[2] This choice goes *beyond* our initial
profession of faith.

This choice is not for the unsaved, those who
have yet to be born again of His Spirit; rather, it
is for those who are *already* of the household of
faith in Christ Jesus. Christians must decide to
get serious about their relationship with Jesus
and their commitment to the Word and Will of God.
It is a decision to forsake the "wilderness", that
merry-go-round existence of unbelief. Finally, it
is the decision to *cross the Jordan* and go on with
God!

Yes, to go *on* with God. Isn't that what being a
Christian is all about? So often I hear precious,
sincere believers make statements like: "I'd love
to have an anointing on my life! I'd love to see lives
changed, to see lives *transformed* around me. I'd
love to see more healings take place, to see the
supernatural power of God manifested."

Well, let me just say that these are all very good
desires. This is what the "Good News" is all about,
isn't it? We want to see lives changed and transformed into the very image and glory of God! Such
anointing as we desire to see, can only come
through consecration to the Word and Will of God.
This anointing can come only by walking up to that
river called the "Jordan" and taking a leap of faith![3]

As children of God, disciples of Jesus, we *must*
commit to those "leaps" of faith from time to time
in order to reach that level of consecration and
anointing that the Lord truly desires for our lives.
And what is consecration? Consecration is that
yearning—that fervent, burning heart-*desire* to

follow Jesus! Consecration is that fervent heart *commitment* to obey the Lord and to be pleasing to Him in every area of our lives. It's not just separation from the world, but separation *unto* God, in an intimate relationship with Him.

The crossing of the Jordan represents nothing more than the battle for the human *heart*. The Jordan River itself, represents a *barrier: any* barrier posed by the world, the flesh or the devil which prevents us from realizing that "Promised Land" of personal relationship with God. Those who speak in faith to that barrier, those who speak in faith to that mountain to be removed and cast into the sea will *cross* Jordan and go on with God.[4] Those who are *fearful* of its torrent, will turn back and go on with *the world.*

The difference in what we do with the Jordan lies in the heart. Whether we brave the Jordan and go on with God or whether we turn back and go on with the world, depends upon our consecration to the Word and Will of God.

When we are born again of the Spirit of God, we should be taught *immediately* that through faith in Jesus as our "Burnt Offering", *we can choose* to receive that joyful heart of consecration. This heart will take us straight to the "rest" of the Promised Land. We can choose *not* to spend years in the wilderness while God purges the world out of our hearts. *We can choose* not to waste so much of our lives struggling to resist the vomit of Egypt, the bitter-sweet delicacies of the world and the pleasures (or bondage) of sin. Through Jesus, we can *cross* the Jordan, that barrier which resists our desire for a deeper walk with God. Through *Jesus* we can forsake the world. Through Jesus we can truly seek the *Kingdom of God* and His righteousness first!

You will find that when God calls upon you to cross your "Jordan," the world will be calling you, as well. When the Lord begins to move in your life, satan will try to distract you. Satan will use the world with all of its delicacies, all of its idols and its "pleasures" to tempt you, to torment you and to do whatever he *has* to do to keep you from crossing Jordan. His attacks are focused on the *heart:* your mind, will and emotions. Satans attacks are focused on the very windows to your soul in an effort to pull you back into Egypt, and thus into the bondage of sin and separation from God.

How do you resist such attack? We can choose to believe God's Word and allow the Power of God to affect victory in our lives.[5] The Apostle Paul had to *choose* to "die daily" to the carnal influences in his life so that the resurrection power of Jesus might be evidenced in his life.[6] *We* therefore, must actively make the decision each and every day to say "no" to the world, to say "no" to the flesh, and to say "no" to the devil! It has got to be a committed act of our own will to say, "World, let go of me; I'm going to cross that Jordan. I'm going on with Jesus! I may not know exactly what's in store for me, but I am going to make a decision based on *faith* in God's Word and His *righteousness.* I am going to make a decision to honor *God* instead of *self,* to glorify Jesus instead of the devil!"

You see, when we live for *self* we will *never* find that place of anointing which God so earnestly desires for our lives: for His church. We *must* choose to take that leap of faith and cross the Jordan. We have *got* to trust God, seek righteousness, and move forward with Jesus! Even when the world curses and ridicules us or it seems there is no profit, from the world's standpoint, we must follow Jesus. We honor God more when we make the commitment to seek Him with all of our heart (stumbling and falling in the process), than when we merely *say* we are living for God (and in reality are living only for *self*). We only *deceive* ourselves when we choose to sit back in our comfort zone, instead of actively choosing to press into the Kingdom on a daily basis.[7]

It takes *courage* to brave the swelling of the Jordan, to go on with Jesus. It takes *cowardice* to remain where we are with no other direction to go but backwards. *Whichever* way we choose, God holds us accountable.[8] Therefore, we should choose to go on and cross the Jordan!

Yes, we all have that choice to make! We *can* be a Ruth, instead of an Orpah. We can choose to be a Timothy instead of a Demas.[9] We *can* be that "good and faithful" servant if we could put away our childish flirtations with the world and *choose Jesus*. Therefore, we must choose! Let's all go down in history as great men and women of God, and not as Reuben, Gad and half the tribe of Manasseh. They chose to live in compromise, to go backward in their relationship with God. They chose to *reject* God's best, His most perfect will for their lives! Therefore, we too must choose whom we will serve. We have the choice to go down in history either in greatness or in mediocrity!

"I call heaven and earth as witnesses today against you, that I have set before you life and death, blessing and cursing; therefore, choose life, that both you and your descendants may live;

That you may love the Lord your God, that you may obey His voice, and that you may cling to Him, for He is your life and the length of your days, and that you may dwell in the land which the Lord swore to your fathers, to Abraham, Isaac, and Jacob, to give them." Deuteronomy 30:19-20

NOTES:

1 Romans 11:29
2 Hebrews 4:1-11
3 Jeremiah 12:5; Joshua 3
4 Matthew 17:20; Luke 17:5-6
5 1 John 5:3-5
6 1 Corinthians 15:31-34
7 Jeremiah 48:11
8 Numbers 32
9 2 Timothy 4:10—Demas, a man who forsook the Apostle Paul having loved the world more than he loved Jesus.

3.

BETWEEN TWO KINGDOMS

"And Elijah came to all the people, and said, "How long will you falter between two opinions? If the Lord is God, follow Him: but if Baal, then follow him. "   **1 Kings 18:21**

A few years ago I was running an exercise studio, encouraging people to stay fit, and at the same time taking drugs in the back room. It was similar to the time I was running a quit-smoking-quick clinic and smoking in the back room. My spiritual life ran a close parallel to my professional life, as what is in your heart ultimately does come out in your daily living.

This was the case one night in the back room of the exercise studio. I claimed to be a Christian during that period of my life. I prayed to God as a Christian. In fact, while I was living a compromised life, I prayed, "Lord, please protect me and forgive me." How deceived I was! What had happened to me was that the deceitfulness of sin (Heb. 3:13) had overtaken me. I longed for the worldly pleasures of sin rather than the eternal rewards of righteousness. My heart was completely blind to God and His ways. The most

sickening thing about it is, I knew it. I knew I was
trampling on the precious blood of Jesus. I was a
"grace-coaster," feeling completely free to enjoy my
sin because all I had to do was ask God to forgive
me and He would . . . or so I had been told.

On that night, however, God not only heard my
prayers, He answered me. In what seemed like an
audible voice although I am sure it was simply
audible to my own mind and heart—God spoke to
me that night as I prepared my little "safety"
prayer.

"Doug," He said, "Don't call me 'Lord' if you will
not do what I say."

Thinking I was being reasonable. I answered
back, "Well, Lord, I know that Jesus is the Son of
God, so I know that means I'm saved."

Again the Lord spoke to my heart, "Doug, even
the demons in Hell know who I am. What makes
you any different?"

This was long before I knew what God had said
in Scripture along the same lines. Coming from
God Himself, it rattled every nerve and bone in my
body. That last statement brought the fear of the
Lord into my life like nothing before. Shaking, and
feeling very alone in that back room, I began to
evaluate where I was in life, my goals and desires,
the entire direction I was taking. God had confronted me. With one simple statement from His
Word, He cut through all the deception of sin in
my heart.

At that point, I realized I had a choice to make,
a choice between two worlds. A choice between
the pleasures of sin for a season or the righteousness of God. A choice between the love of the world
and the fear of the Lord. Sitting in that little room,
I made my choice. I chose Jesus. I chose to love

Him with all my heart, with all my soul and with all my might. It was a tough choice, even tougher to follow through with it. But it was the right choice, the only choice if I wanted to live beyond my spiritual schizophrenic existence. That encounter with a living God marked a turning point in my life.

Somehow, in the days and months to come, God forged out of my life a ministry to lost and confused people like I had been. A ministry that came to be known as "Turning Point Ministries." Slowly, the evening exercise classes became nights of prayer. The studio became a place for teams of us to meet before launching out onto the street to witness. Finally I had to close the exercise studio, and I was launched into the greatest adventure of my life: learning to live by faith! Various churches helped us out. Church crowd met street crowd. Some churches turned us away. Some who I would have thought were just "pew-warming" Christians warmly embraced us, offering their very livelihood to help rehabilitate those outcasts who were meeting the Savior for a turning point in their lives. Others simply did not want to be bothered. Through those months, the difference between the Christian world and the secular world was deeply impressed on my mind and heart. For me, for those to whom I ministered, and for those who helped us, there was no middle ground.

The two worlds really are two spiritual kingdoms. The Kingdom of God is righteousness, and the kingdom of Satan is the love of the world and all that is contrary to righteousness. The Lord showed me through the various people I met that it is possible to live in both worlds, with a foot in the spiritual and one in the world. But when it

comes time for God to call His children home, the
straddlers won't be going. The "secular" world
includes the streets (the "worldly" world) but also
includes some who call "Lord, Lord" like I had.

Jesus said that God's children cannot serve
both God and mammon.[1] "Mammon" is a figurative word for "the world." It means "confidence,
i.e., figurative of wealth, personified: avarice
(deified)." It connotes a world that puts its confidence in material wealth and in the seeking of
that wealth. It connotes avarice, which is
covetousness and greed. It is described as wealth
"personified" because "personified" means to at-
tribute a human character or "personhood" to an
inanimate object or concept. It is avarice "deified"
because "deified" means to make something into
a god and worship it as such. In other words,
mammon is the material world and all it has to
offer, placed in a position of being worshipped as
a god. Jesus uses "mammon" to illustrate how
wealth itself is exalted to the place which should
be occupied by God. No wonder we cannot serve
both at the same time.

We cannot serve two gods. We cannot serve
God and also serve sin. We cannot seek what is
of interest in the world and still please God, because what is of interest in the world is not of
interest to God. What is cherished by the world is
an abomination to God.[2] *It is impossible to love
the One without hating the other, and impossible
to hold the other, without despising the One.* We
cannot embrace the covetousness and greed of the
world and at the same time embrace the
righteousness of God. People are kidding themselves when they pray little prayers but refuse to
turn their lives over to God. People on the pews

do the same.

Two worlds of such opposite character and purpose simply cannot be reconciled. The only way to reconcile yourself to two kingdoms of two different natures is to choose between them.

There are those who have tried to avoid that choice. The Church at Laodicea was denounced by Christ in the book of Revelation. "Because you are lukewarm I will spew you out of my mouth," Jesus said.

For the last two years I have taken ministry trips to Vietnam and Southeast Asia with a team of veterans and ministers. During one of my trips I became desperately ill. The doctors warned about an amoeba, Malaria or Typhoid, which I know other people have died from. All I know is that my body was fighting desperately to get something out of it. After a lot of prayer, I finally received a clean bill of health.

What I experienced must be what God meant when He said He wanted to vomit up lukewarmness! Lukewarmness makes God sick. Everything within Him wants to rid Himself of it. Yet, many professing Christians are worshiping the god of self and this world. By doing so, they are despising the Lord. They are making His Body ache and writhe in pain.

Lukewarmness comes over us gradually. First you are "hot" and "on fire" for God, then the process of justifying and rationalizing sin takes place. When truth is finally shoved aside, you become friends with the world and are no longer hot or cold, but lukewarm.

We know that our very bodies are the temple of the Holy Spirit on earth today.[3] Each time we put our trust in this world and its devices to sustain

us, we place the temple of the Holy Spirit in
bondage to a Satanic world system. By pursuing
worldly relationships and possessions, we become
idolators and worshipers of the world. Obviously
this "lukewarmness" cannot be acceptable to a
Holy God.

This was so clear to me upon coming home from
Vietnam. The poverty and oppression of the
general populace, and the squalid conditions at
orphanages were thrown in sharp relief to the
spiritual riches of persecuted Christians. They
are more hungry for God than for their scarcely
adequate food. Under threat of their lives they
meet, baptize, worship and teach others about
God. And with joy! To come home after my first
trip and try to express these findings to a blessed
and apathetic people in a "free" world was one of
the most trying times of my ministry.

Just before His denunciation of Laodicea, Jesus
lauded the Church of Smyrna saying, "I know
your works, tribulation and poverty (but you are
so rich)."[4] This is so true of the Christians of
Vietnam today. But for Christians of abundantly
blessed nations I can hear Jesus saying, "You say
I am rich, have become wealthy, and have need of
nothing and do not know that you are wretched,
miserable, poor, blind and naked."[5] It is so easy
to become naked and poor in the midst of physical
comforts and riches. May God's mercy be with
those who do. "To whom much is given. much is
required."[6]

The choice must be made. The loving and
compassionate Jesus, Who laid down His life for
us on the cross of Calvary is the very same Who
says He will vomit us out of His mouth if we are
found to be "lukewarm" through comfortable com-

promise with the world. He leaves no room for "Carnal Christianity." In Fact, "Carnal Christianity" is a self-delusion. It's just another way of saying, "I want to live for the world, but I also want to be accepted by God. I want to partake of the pleasures of sin, but I also want 'fire insurance.'" Either we are disciples of Christ or we are not. Either we love God or are at enmity with Him. Jesus loved us so much that He voluntarily laid down His life and poured out His blood for us, choosing to be separated from God during that climactic moment on the Cross if it meant to be united with us for all of eternity. What love! How can we return to Him less than a genuinely yielded life?

Whatever we choose, there are consequences to our choice. Proverbs 13:13 says, "He who despises the word will be destroyed, but he who fears the commandment will be rewarded." God makes His point pretty clear! There are consequences for despising the Word of God. When truth is shoved aside and His commandments are ignored, we bring destruction upon ourselves. When we continue to set our affections between two worlds and persistently walk in compromise with God we will be "destroyed." But, obedience brings great reward and yields the peaceable fruit of righteousness (Ezek. 14:13-14).

What is God doing in the midst of all this compromise? He desires such communion with us that He continues to reach out to us. Through His loving judgements, God is bringing us to a place where we are willing and able to walk with Him in oneness of heart, oneness of soul, oneness of mind and oneness of Spirit. As this is carried out, we will come to the place where people will

see the distinction in our lives. We are different
in values, the way we act, how we do business.
Our lives indeed become different—holy,
separated to God.

Either we receive His instruction and reap His
rewards, or we despise His instruction and reap
His judgements. Either we cross the Jordan and
enter into His rest, or we wander in a wilderness,
our indecision making our decision for us.

There are, then, two distinct kingdoms or
worlds. A person does not have to be a Satanist,
as many of our young people are today, to be a
follower of the kingdom of satan. One simply
needs to choose NOT to live in the Kingdom of God,
and one's address is automatically in the other
kingdom.

"I beseech you therefore, brethren, by the mer-
cies of God, that you present your bodies a living
sacrifice, holy, acceptable to God, which is your
reasonable service. And do not be conformed to
this world, but be transformed by the renewing of
your mind, that you may prove what is that good
and acceptable and perfect will of God."[7]

NOTES:

[1] Matt. 6:24
[2] Luke 16:15
[3] 1 Cor. 6:19
[4] Rev. 2:9
[5] Rev. 3:17
[6] Luke 12:48
[7] Rom. 12:1-2

4.

PROPHETIC DRAMA

Ten years ago when "Turning Point" was still meeting in the exercise studio, Greg came in one night for the exercise class and prayer. I later moved in with Greg out of his generosity while the ministry was still forming. There were more strange people in and out of that apartment during those months than either of us can remember! In fact, I remember one Christmas season having taken in the apartment 17 people, ranging from runaways, drug addicts, prostitutes and children wanting help. In addition I had people staying in the exercise studio and in a widow friend's home.

Greg and I have alternately blessed each other and frustrated each other. But time has proven the unique bond God placed between us during that period of our lives. Times of prayer, spiritual warfare, and caring for others side by side had made us truly closer than brothers.

So I was filled with almost tearful joy a few years ago when Greg called me and told me of his impending marriage to Christy. One day as he was praising God in his room, he suddenly sensed the Lord speak to his heart about Christy. He knew Christy from a Bible study he attended, but never looked at her as a potential wife. He went to his pastor and asked him about it. Come to find out, the Lord had revealed to the pastor that Greg and Christy were to be married, and Christy had already pondered these things prior to this, saying God had told her the same thing.

Following a whirlwind engagement, they were married in a gloriously inspired ceremony. To say I was happy is an understatement. But underneath my happiness was a sadness, almost a jealousy, that God had not done for me what He did for Greg. I live with people almost constantly surrounding me, but there is always the awareness that no one is "special" to me, no wife is there to support me, sharing the vision with me.

I was in this frame of mind when I fell into a relationship with a woman that was to last some years. She was beautiful (they always are!), intelligent, capable, from a wealthy family, and she desired to follow Jesus. But no matter what I did, she continued to have her doubts. Through it all, she never understood my love, never grasped what I knew God wanted and could do through her.

But I didn't see all that. I saw a few setbacks, sure, but that was to be expected. In every way, she was perfect for me. Having experience in managing business and people, she would be a natural helpmeet to the ministry. She loved and wanted children and, I believed, she loved and wanted me. Everything was perfect. Or so I thought. This became a time when the Lord allowed me to experience some heart-rending struggles—some deep emotional hurts that I would be hard-pressed to express in words. In fact, it was one of the worst emotional trials of my life.

I was devastated, completely debilitated. It

seemed my whole life had crumbled and my heart ripped out. I could hardly function for days. A friend who was wounded in Vietnam tells of constant nightmares of pain and memories. Likewise, the pain and memories of this relationship haunted me at every turn and seemed impossible to overcome. Each day I battled thoughts of her. Just as my friend had to have his wounds cleansed in the hospital, I needed the cleansing power of God to bring healing in my life. How that hurts! There is nothing more debilitating than a broken or wounded heart. I wonder how Jesus thinks of us? Does He experience the pain and heartache each time we dishonor Him and break His heart?

God used this period of my life. As a result of my experience, I can better understand the pain which God feels in His heart for His Church. He spoke to me through the circumstances. He showed me how the church doesn't really understand the depth of God's love and compassion for us. When Jesus hung on the cross to die, His heart was broken. It felt like it was ripping out of His body. What does He think of us now after having made that ultimate sacrifice and suffering a broken heart? Are we constantly in His thoughts? His Word says we are. Does He experience pain as we dishonor and disobey Him? His Word says He does. He looks at us like a jealous lover, wanting us to realize the greatness of His love for us and turn ourselves toward Him.

I believe God allowed me to go through that painful experience as a lesson to me. I believe He allows us to experience that kind of hurt and rejection at times in our walk with Him to give us a small understanding of that part of Him—His supreme love and compassion.

During this trial, I feel as if I personally felt in a small way, God's emotions for the Church, His love for the "Bride of Christ." How awesome it is! How overwhelming it is! How magnificent! Yet, we continue to walk away from His warmth, His covering, and from His precious care because we think that we can do things better our way. How foolish!

It breaks my heart now to see the shortcomings of my own life, much less the lives of those I love. I want everyone I love to see the spiritual and eternal aspect of things, not just the physical and temporal. God wants so much for us to set our hearts on Him, rather than the things of this world.[1] His Holy Spirit pleads with us to come to God that we might have life, and even have it more abundantly.[2] Yet, we continue to spurn and reject Him.

True ministry, God's ministry, goes much deeper than simple verbal expression and platitudes. In the ministry which God has entrusted me, many of the people really don't know or realize the prayer, the intercession or the time spent on the knees weeping for their souls. They don't see the investment sown spiritually for them.

Likewise, there are groups of people, our ministry included, who are weeping for the Church; spending hours on their knees in intercession; crying out for the hurt that the Church has heaped on its Creator. Meanwhile, the Church walks in indifference to a loving God. Many people, even in the institution of the Church do not comprehend the depth of God's desire for personal communion with them. He breathed His life into us—His very own Spirit!

Shortly after my heart had broken, I was scheduled to a city-wide rally in Conroe, Texas. For whatever reason, the school board allowed a group of churches to hold the meeting in a high school auditorium. I had been excited about it before, but now I didn't want to go. I didn't want to be around people, much less talk to people, much less talk to a bunch of people! But there I was. As I climbed onto the stage, my heart heavy, I knew I had to tell these young people the Truth.

"My heart is broken today," I started. Then I told them about the Prophetic Drama the Lord allowed me to experience. My life experience became the message. Ultimately, the message of God's heart for this generation and His Church. This crowd of young people settled right down and hung on every word. They identified with the sense of rejection, pains and heartache.

"Many of you have felt a little like this," I said. "And no one likes it. But what about God? How does He feel? God loves you so much He let His Son die for you, and what are you doing to Him in return? Mocking Him? Rejecting Him? Listening to Satanic music, watching perverted music videos and following anti-Christ teachers?" There was a swell of them at the front wanting to commit themselves to Christ following the meeting. It was an incredible event!

A few days later, I took a plane to a conference. I hadn't eaten for days and the peanuts the flight steward offered turned my stomach just to look at them. Then the Lord spoke to me inside, like He had in the gym years earlier. He said He knew that I felt like giving up. It was true. I was ready to drop everything, go find a job somewhere and live like a hermit for the rest of my life.

Then God showed me how badly people feel who do not have Him. They suffer so much that they escape into drugs, alcohol, promiscuous sex, businesses, the things of this world that will not last, and even suicide.

After showing me the despair of the world—and believe me I was totally depressed already and this didn't help—God reminded me of what He had been saying, that Jesus felt this way on the cross. And, because He overcame it, I would too.

The power of the resurrection of Christ was going to pull me through this! With those words God began to heal me. I was healed as I recognized the pain He Himself overcame when Christ was resurrected from the grave, no longer dead and hanging on a cross, but gloriously raised—alive!

The prophet Hosea had a wife who was adulterous and unfaithful. Likewise, the Bride of Christ, the Church, spurns and rejects the Bridegroom's love to follow after other things more important to her. Jesus actively courts the Church, but the Church does not respond. There are individuals within the Church who say they love Him, but He agonizes because their hearts are divided with the world. We simply cannot have friendships with the world, for it is the enemy of God.

How long will God's Holy Spirit contend with us? How long will we be unfaithful, not heeding His voice? We have rejected God's servants, therefore we rejected Him. We have crushed those who spoke to instruct us. God hears their cries and will vindicate them. I am as guilty as anyone of trampling God's grace under my feet.

We say we are willing to serve Him, but where is our action? We say we love Him but only give

Him tokens of our time. We spend time socially with those who call on His Name, but have no depth in our hearts to heed His voice. The Church lives in two worlds! God has warned us, but because of our divided heart we ignore Him. As in the days of Noah, calamity will fall on those who are satisfied with their own mediocrity.

The enemy comes suddenly as a "friend," in order to drag us back into the world. If we cater to the delicacies of those who are not Christ's disciples, the enemy will bring us low. Satan comes as an angel of light. Our only protection is to obey God's Words and find refuge in them. Only in God is there power to destroy the works of the devil. God's Word is a lamp unto our feet and a light unto our path.[3] but only when we use it! We are often like spiritual sluggards who have a spiritual feast before us, but can't even pick up a spoon to eat.[4]

It is time more of us in the Church crossed the Jordan, leaving everything behind, and following the Lord. It is time more of us concentrate on God's broken heart and do everything we can to give Him the love and obedience He deserves, to make His heart glad and joyful at our devotion to Him.

NOTES:

[1] Col. 3:1-2
[2] John 10:10
[3] Ps 119:105
[4] Prov.26:15

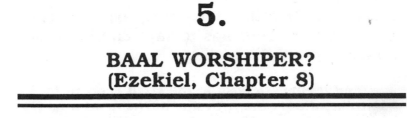

5.

BAAL WORSHIPER?
(Ezekiel, Chapter 8)

To the Christian, the Baal god is *anything* that masters or possesses our affections above Jesus Christ. Ezekiel was God's spokesman to an exiled church: a church that had been exiled to the "wilderness" of *Babylon*, that civilization which is so typical of our society today. Ezekiel was also a *watchman* to the house of Israel. He "watched over" a stiffnecked and rebellious people who were wholly inclined toward *idolatry*. This inclination rendered Israel totally susceptible to the seductions of a pagan environment.

This particular period in Israel's history represents a remarkable parallel to the history of the church today. We also, live in a corrupt, pagan environment, and are wholly inclined toward idolatry. We are susceptible to the sinful seductions around us. However, instead of a man like Ezekiel to "watch over" us, God has sent His own Holy Spirit "to accomplish that task"—to reprove the world of sin and of righteousness and of judgement.[1]

The name "Ezekiel" means "God strengthens." The Holy Spirit can and is using the message of

Ezekiel to strengthen the hand of the church today, just as He used it to convict and strengthen the House of Israel in the past. Therefore, let us also listen to the words of a man who grieved over the seductions of his people. Let us also listen to the conviction of the Holy Spirit as we open our hearts to the light of His Word. As we study the message of Ezekiel, let us truly be concerned about what the Lord has to say concerning our relationship with Him today.

> *"And it came to pass in the sixth year, in the sixth month, on the fifth day of the month, as I sat in my house with the elders of Judah sitting before me, that the hand of the Lord God fell upon me there.*
> *Then I looked, and there was a likeness, like the appearance of fire-from the appearance of His waist and downward, fire; and from His waist and upward, like the appearance of brightness, like the color of amber.*
> *He stretched out the form of a hand, and took me by a lock of my hair; and the Spirit lifted me up between earth and heaven, and brought me in visions of God to Jerusalem, to the door of the north gate of the inner court, where the seat of the image of jealousy was, which provokes to jealousy."*   Ezekiel 8:1-3

Okay, so let's get the picture as to what is happening here. Ezekiel is sitting in his house preaching, praying and/or conferring with the "Elders of Judah." Judah means *praise*. The "Elders of Judah" here, are representative of the church as a whole (which is supposed to be the praise and glory of God on the earth). However, particular attention is drawn to the *elders* of Judah, in other words, to the *leadership* of the church! Obviously, God is giving Ezekiel a vision to share with the leadership, a vision which is designed to convict them of their sin. Upon *conviction*, they are to minister to the people that self-same repentance.

Ezekiel is transported in this vision to the inner court of the temple itself. In the inner court is an *image of jealousy*. It's an image which provokes a jealous God to jealousy for the affections of His people! This image represents an idol or the sin of idolatry amongst the people. Just as Israel was guilty of worshiping idols in God's own temple, so is the *church* guilty of harboring idolatry in the heart, in the temple of God's Holy Spirit today. Do you know what? *God is jealous!*

> *And behold, the glory of the God of Israel was there, like the vision that I saw in the plain.*
>
> *Then He said to men, "Son of man, lift your eyes now toward the north," So I lifted my eyes toward the north, and there, north of the altar gate, was this image of jealousy in the entrance.*
>
> *Furthermore He said to me, "Son of man, do you see what they are doing, the great abominations that the house of Israel commits here, to make Me go far away from My sanctuary? Now turn again, you will see greater abominations." Ezekiel 8:4-6*

What is it that Israel is doing here? Sure, they are worshiping an idol, but is that all? The Lord is taking great pains here to detail exactly where this idol is located within the temple! Where this idol is located will help us to understand what is particularly offensive about this form of idolatry. Look at verses 3-5 again, but especially at verse 5. Notice the mention of "the north" or "northward" over and over again. The north side of the altar is typical of judgement:[2] judgement such as only God can give, and specifically, the judgement which has been rendered against *sin*.

This is why the Levitical sacrifices were always
offered on the north side of the altar.[3] Jesus
Himself being the absolute fulfillment *of* those
sacrifices, was offered up on the *north side* of
Jerusalem which of course, represented God's
final judgement against sin!

So what is the importance of this in our discus-
sion?   Well, think about it!   Israel has set up
another god in the House of the Lord. This other
god does *not* know the judgement against sin.
They set up this idol   *in the place of* or   *in
preeminence* to the accepted *altar* of God (which is
Jesus) where sin is finally judged and dealt with
within our hearts.   Therefore, if the people are
worshiping at the feet of an idol which knows not
the righteousness of the Lord, then they are worshiping at the altar of *sin*.   Likewise, if we are
preferring this "image of jealousy" before the image
of God in Christ Jesus, then we have not the
reflection of *Jesus in our lives*; but rather, we have
the reflection of the idolatrous world in which we
live!

Do you see it?   God is saying here that we have
preferred the idolatrous worship of the world over
the holy altar of God where our sins are dealt with.
Instead, we seek the temporal pleasures of this
world. We have ceased to humble ourselves before
God. We no longer lay our sins upon His altar that
they may be judged; we choose to seek our own
desires.   In doing so, we have become like the
adulterous woman of Proverbs 30:20. Because
she sins then wipes her mouth, saying, "I have
done no wrong," she has become a figure of the sin
of *spiritual* adultery.   This sin is notorious for
having an outward "form" of godliness, but which
has no fear of God *in the heart.*

Again, we may not be doing anything *outwardly* sinful, but we are committing sexual immorality in the spirit when our hard hearts are not totally yielded to the Lord. Thus, when it comes to making Godly decisions in our lives, we choose the *ungodly*. When we should give God *all* of our heart, we say "not right now, Lord, there are other things that I would like to accomplish, first."

Oh, how the church needs to understand the depth of the fear of the Lord! We need to stop pushing God out of His House, out of our own lives, so that once again, He can anoint us with *His* power and *His* glory.

> **7 So He brought me to the door of the court; and when I looked, there was a hole in the wall.**
>
> **8 Then He said to me, "Son of man, dig into the wall"; and when I dug into the wall, there was a door.**
>
> **9 And He said to me, "Go in, and see the wicked abominations which they are doing there."**
>
> **10 So I went in and saw, and there—every sort of creeping thing, abominable beasts, and all the idols of the house of Israel, portrayed all around on the walls.** Ezekiel 8:7-10

There are just two things which I would like to point out about this passage. First, remember God is talking about the *church* here, not about the ungodly. Second, Ezekiel 8:10, states that the church, *His people*, are involved in every form of idolatry and sin that the *ungodly* are involved in. In other words, there is no distinction between the children of God and the children of the world in God's eyes; they have become one in heart as well as deed. Instead of pursuing the righteousness of God, the church is pursuing the unrighteousness of mammon.

The spiritual state of Israel therefore, had become totally compromised through the seductions of the pagan environment in which they lived. It happened because of their own lust of the flesh, lust of the eyes and pride of life.[4] The Lord allowed Ezekiel to see into this secret chamber of God's own house; it was a chamber in which the Elders of Israel sought to hide their inner thoughts and secret sins from the Lord. Just like Ezekiel, we ought to look within the secret chambers of our own hearts! We need to search out what is really within *our* temples! What do we really see painted on the walls of our own hearts? Do we see bold and uncompromised stands for the Lord? Are we disciples willing to receive shame, ridicule, humiliation, or persecution at school, on the job or within the marketplace? Do we see disciples who are unashamed of the Gospel, willing to lay down our lives for the Name of Jesus Christ? Or, are we possibly seeing all manner of filth and uncleanliness which is characteristic of the children of this idolatrous world?

> *11 And there stood before them seventy men of the elders of the house of Israel, and in their midst stood Jaazaniah the son of Shaphan. Each man had a censer in his hand, and a thick cloud of incense went up.*
> *12 Then He said to me, "Son of man, have you seen what the elders of the house of Israel do in the dark, every man in the room of his idols? For they say, 'The Lord does not see us, the Lord has forsaken the land.'"*
> *13 And He said to me, "Turn again, and you will see greater abominations that they are doing."*   *Ezekiel 8:11-13*

In Ezekiel 8 verse 11, the symbolical number of "70" confirms our contention that these "Ancients of Israel," though representative of the leadership specifically, are also representative of the church as a whole. God is simply saying here that the spiritual state of the leadership will *always* be mirrored by the people to whom they are required to be examples! Thus, in verses 11 and 12, we see the Lord comparing what the church is actively doing as opposed to what is really in their hearts.[5]

On the one hand, the church is offering up prayers as if they are in right relationship with God[6] (verse 11). On the other hand, because they are spiritual adulterers in heart, they are actually *doing* all manner of wickedness in their flesh, "in the dark." "In the dark" means that they are doing these things *in secret*. They deceive themselves by thinking that the Lord neither sees, nor cares about their sins. These elders think that the Lord is altogether like their idols; they don't see Him as a *Holy God*. He is seen as subject to *their* control and to their own desires. These people have no *fear* of God and are unable to comprehend the *Holiness* of God. This prevents them from giving their *hearts* to God.

> **14 So He brought me to the door of the north gate of the Lord's house; and to my dismay, women were sitting there weeping for Tammuz.**
> **15 Then He said to me, "Have you seen this, O son of man? Turn again, you will see greater abominations than these."   Ezekiel 8:14-15**

There is a significant progression here which we need to look at. Notice the recurring phrases in verses 6, 13 and now in verse 15. The Lord is showing us the natural progression of the effects of sin in our lives; the sin leads to greater and greater abominations! As stated before, the compromised walk is a *gradual* process; it doesn't just happen all at once. The Lord shows us how this occurs.

For example, sin *begins* in the heart; it is called *iniquity*. In this case, the house of Israel had replaced their affections for the Lord and *His* righteousness, with the idolatrous affections of the world—a world which knows *not* "judgement" against sin. From here, God says, "Turn again and you shall see greater abominations." (verses 5 and 6)

In verse 6 we saw that the house of Israel pushed the Lord out of His sanctuary through the spiritual adultery that was in their hearts. Now, in verses 7 through 12, we see them refilling the sanctuary of their heart and mind. Because the Lord has been removed, their sanctuary becomes a *spiritual vacuum*. This is an inward manifestation of the physical idol (image of jealousy) that Israel had raised up in the House of God. They are now embellishing this idol as they fill their "sanctuary" with all manner of filth, uncleanliness, impure thoughts and desires. (verse 10)

Now begin the *visible* stages of the compromised walk—hypocrisy. What began in the heart, becomes only a *form* of godliness. That which was done in secret will now be known outwardly! The church is continuing the pretense of prayer and right relationship with God while engaged in all manner of wickedness. (verses 11-12) *Hypocrisy!* The fact that they were doing these things in secret is evidence that the children of Israel knew what they were doing was wrong. God's people *willfully chose* to rebel against their Creator!

In verse 14 we see the final stages of rebellion against God. Now the heart continues to be deceived and hardened through hypocrisy and begins to make a more outward show of its affection (verse 14). With this outward show of affection, open rebellion against God is not far behind. (verse 16-17)

In verse 14, we see the "women of God" weeping for Tammuz, the Babylonian god of worldly desire. The worship of Tammuz was connected with *Licentiousness*, partying or orgy-type festivals. Licentiousness (taking license) means loose, lustful or lawless behavior. The women of God were *weeping* for this personification of worldly desire! They had exalted this desire to the place of *godhead* within their hearts. Deep down they wanted to be lustful, to be loose and lawless of spirit. They also knew that this heart attitude *offended* a three times Holy God! The women of God wanted "the world" and at the same time, wanted to worship in the House of God. Since they couldn't have it both ways, they had to make a choice! This choice tore apart their soul and left them weeping for their god, Tammuz.

How many of us weep for Tammuz in the very same way? We are serving God while our souls are literally torn apart by the lusts of this world. How many of us actually *desire* to be loose, lawless, and lustful of spirit, deep down in our hearts? Is God well-pleased with such a heart? Of course not! If the *desire* is there, then there is an idol in our heart that needs to be *utterly destroyed!* That idol (sin) needs to be placed at the foot of the cross and left there!

If our minds are not totally subjected to the Holy Spirit, and if our hearts are not totally given to God and set apart for His use, then be assured that we *will fall prey* to the spirit of this age—that licentious worship of worldly desire! Now more than ever, we need to understand that we are in the presence of a *jealous* God. If we do not want to be thrown up and suffer His loving wrath, we had better sell out and live in *one* world, *His* world!

How many of us have loved the Lord in the past but became seduced by this world? It happened because of the idolatry in our own hearts. How many of us had to hit *rock bottom* before we realized the "lukewarmness" of our relationship with Him? We literally felt "thrown up", didn't we? Well, God did *not* forsake us as we all tend to think at times. *We* forsake Him and He allows His righteous judgement because of His boundless love toward us. He so wants us to be brought back into that intimate relationship with Him.

> *16 So He brought me into the inner court of the Lord's house; and there, at the door of the temple of the Lord, between the porch and the altar, were about about twenty-five men with their backs toward the temple of the Lord and their faces toward the east, and they were worshiping the sun toward the east.*
>
> *17 Then He said to me, "Have you seen this, O son of man? Is it a trivial thing to the house of Judah to commit the abominations which they commit here? For they have filled the land with violence; then they have returned to provoke Me to anger. Indeed they put the branch to their nose.*
>
> *18 Therefore, I also will act in fury. My eye will not spare nor will I have pity; and though they cry in My ears with a loud voice, I will not hear them."*   *Ezekiel 8:16-18*

Here we see the final result of the choice which Israel has made; Israel went from idolatry in the heart to open worship of a strange god in God's own House (verse 16). These twenty-five men, in

fact, are worshiping Baal, the sun god, *as* God.[7]
Baal means "Lord, possessor, husband;" therefore, Baal is the lord of their lives. The children of
Israel also partake of all the immoral idolatry that
Baal is connected with. Baal is the possessor of
their souls; he is their husband. Jehovah, who
betrothed them to Himself has been replaced by
another god.

Because Baal is their Lord, they are worshiping
him in full view of all Israel. The children of Israel
are totally unashamed of their actions. This is the
natural progression of iniquity in the heart, total
and outright rebellion against God!

Likewise, in our own lives, God loves us enough
to warn us. He warns us of the false teachers in
the church and the ministering wolves in the
pulpit. He warns us of "children of God" who, by
their *lifestyle*, openly deny the Deity and Lordship
of Jesus Christ. They openly tolerate the sin of
homosexuality, fornication, adultery, abortion,
and the love of money rather than the love of God.[8]
God is warning us that this is a growing rebellion.
For this reason, He has allowed some idolaters in
the church to be exposed, in order that we may
put a stop to it.

Ending this idolatrous rebellion begins with
each and every one of us. We must ask ourselves
some pretty tough questions and get some honest
answers. Do we spend more time worshiping the
"sun," than worshiping the Son? Do we spend the
majority of our time "sun" bathing, working on our
physical body; our intellect, building up our businesses, pursuing temporal dreams? Are we
spending more time doing the things which satisfy
a loose, lawless and lustful spirit in our hearts?
Or, do we spend the majority of our time seeking

the "Kingdom first and *His* righteousness?" Do we
spend our time praying, studying, worshiping the
Lord in spirit and in truth? Instead, do we spend
time watching T.V., listening to the radio or even
Christian music tapes?

What kind of quality time do we give to a jealous
God? This is the question! How much time do we
spend on our knees seeking Grace from God to
repent of our sins? Reading a few scriptures and
mumbling a few prayers at mealtime and bedtime
just will not get it anymore. We need to repent.
Revival starts here, in the heart of every person!
Obviously, no Christian would admit to being a
Baal worshiper. However, as stated at the beginning of this chapter, Baal worship consists of any
thing that masters or possesses our affections
above that of Jesus Christ. Therefore, with this in
mind, in what areas of our lives have we been Baal
worshipers? There are areas in our lives where,
admittedly, we are Baal worshipers. We must
pray for God's mercy, strength, and grace to overcome those Baal areas of our lives. We must first
accept the fact that we are sinners; we are sick of
spirit in some areas. There are areas that need to
be dealt with, as individuals and as a church.
When we can accept this, we are at the place where
God can bring refreshing!

NOTES:

[1] John16:8
[2] Isaiah 14:13; Psalm 48:1-2; Isaiah 33:5
[3] Leviticus 1:11; Exodus 26:35; 2 Kings 16:14
[4] 1 John 2:15-17
[5] Psalm 51:6
[6] The burning of incense is symbolic of prayer—

Rev. 5:8
7 The number "25" is indicative of a growing rebellion within the church and not one has, as yet, totally possessed the church.
8 It is interesting to note that these are the same sins which were typical of ancient ritual rites connected with the worship of Baal.

6.

THE MARK OF THE LORD
(Ezekiel, Chapter 9)

I can remember a time when the Lord had a few of us place gospel tracts on all the parked cars outside of a topless bar. In fact, night after night for about two weeks we felt the leading to do so. We began interceding and binding the forces of darkness that had the patrons and employees trapped and blinded.

A few months later as I was leasing out apartments to make extra income for the ministry, two young ladies came in to possibly rent. After finding out that they were Christians, I asked them about their testimonies. To my surprise!, Genie, one of the ladies, told me that although she had at one time known of the Lord, she had been working in a topless bar as a bar maid when she kept getting Christian literature on her car. She said that this lasted for about a two week period. Finally one night, after reading about the consequences of sin, she admitted that she was heading straight for Hell and needed a Savior to forgive her sins. As it turns out she had received the literature the same time frame we had been passing them out and at the same topless bar. Praise God!

Learning of the consequences of sin gives us a respectful and healthy expectation of things to come—which is good! The Bible says the fear of the Lord is the beginning of knowledge.[1] If we want to be wise, we need to begin to fear God in a healthy way. To fear God means to hate evil as much as He hates it.[2]. When we hate sin enough to reject it and return to the Father's arms, we find Him ready to embrace us and celebrate our homecoming.

As certain as we are that God loves us, we are also certain of His judgements. Throughout His Word, He repeatedly promises to judge the world, so we believe it! But reading about judgement is never easy. It makes us uncomfortable, and uneasy lest we be guilty of something deserving judgement ourselves. It is not the Lord's will that we would perish,[3] but we bring judgement on ourselves through exercising our own free will and thus rejecting Him.

It is God's holiness that requires judgement to fall upon us. The only way to escape this is if we place that sin under the blood of Jesus through repentance. Christ's sacrifice of Himself pays what we should have paid. We must get our sins "under the blood" because righteous judgement must and surely will come.

Ezekiel is one of the greatest "judgement" prophets. At the time Ezekiel was called out by God to prophesy, the nation of Israel had sinned so badly God banished them from their homeland and they were living in exile in a foreign land. Their number one sin: idolatry. Perhaps that is why Ezekiel strikes a familiar chord with the Church today. Like Israel, the Church today has made decisions to seek after "things," rather than the person of the Lord Jesus. It is simply a modern form of idolatry.

The ninth chapter of Ezekiel has been inspirational as I have meditated on it and preached it to others. When we bathe our words in love— "speaking the truth in love," as the Bible says— then people understand that what we are saying is for their own good. When we had left the tracts on Genie's car, she came to understand our care and concern for her as a person that led us to warn her about the wrong path she had taken. Likewise, God out of His love, tells Ezekiel what is to come and how people can avoid it. And Ezekiel out of love, writes straight from the mouth of God the oracles of God.

"Let those who have charge over the city draw near, each with a deadly weapon in his hand."
Ezekiel 9:1

Ezekiel says God's troops are being mobilized. In the next verse, six men with battle axes come to stand by the bronze altar. This is the altar where animal sacrifices were made before Christ sacrificed Himself, making unnecessary any further sacrifices. Therefore, the bronze altar is symbolic; symbolic of the place where the final sacrifice was made—the cross of Christ.

MARK OF THE LORD OR MARK OF THE BEAST

and the Lord said to him, "Go through the midst of the city, through the midst of Jerusalem, and put a mark on the foreheads of the men who sigh and cry over all the abominations that are done within it.   Ezekiel 9:4

This raises an interesting question. How do we know if we are truly marked with the blood of Christ? How do we know if we are truly marked

with the thoughts and character of a three times
holy God? Are we marked simply because we
profess to be Christians, because of the church we
belong to or because we participate in all of our
church's activities? Are we marked by the blood
of JESUS simply because we carry around a Bible?
Maybe and maybe not!

The point I'm trying to make here may find its
best example in a recent news event. Not too long
ago our tax dollars were used to help fund an art
contest. One of the winning entries was a portrait
that depicted JESUS, our three times holy God, in
a bucket of urine. At one young adult night club,
where we were doing some street ministry and
witnessing the love of JESUS, they were showing
a video of the crucifixion of our Lord with people
performing sex acts behind it. I'm sure you would
agree that these things are pretty disgusting!
Have we become so desensitized that reports such
as this don't really affect us anymore? Who will
rise up and cry out, "I can't take it anymore!?" You
see, it's not only what we may do against God that
is shameful, but what we DON'T DO to stand for
HIS honor. Have we become conditioned to believe
THE LIE with the mark of the beast in our minds?
Are we to be judged for settling into complacency,
as spoken of in Zephaniah 1:12 or for our sins of
omission as in the book of Obadiah?

The significance behind the Mark of the Beast
is what it represents to us. Many would say that
they would never allow the number of the Beast
(666) to be placed upon their foreheads, but I
believe that contrary to popular opinion, the mark
is already being conditioned in the minds of our
generation. The Mark of the Beast represents a
LIE that JESUS CHRIST does not have the right

to be Lord over our lives. We must serve Him first and foremost because of *who* He is, not because of *what* He can do. The Lie therefore, does not place JESUS as the sole Lord over our lives. The Lie is manifest in the lives of many who become the lord of their own lives, by what they believe, by how they live, by how they talk, in the choices and decisions they make, in how they regard others, in the kind of things they allow into their minds and spirit and even the places they feel comfortable going. With whatever mark we are marked, we will show that marking to all of those who are around us, whether it is a marking unto righteousness or a marking unto unrighteousness. The real significance is not the number of the Beast itself, but who we yield ourselves to as Lord—completely. Who is the Lord of our lives? Is it self or the pleasures of this world? If so, satan has conditioned his marking in the mind already.

May we seek the mind of Christ and not be marked with the mind of this world. Again, our minds may not actually be stamped with the number 666, however our minds are being conditioned to live the rebellion and the deception which that mark represents!

JESUS loves us so much that He died for us. He marked us with His very own blood. Therefore, we either live for the Lord, or we live for self. We cannot continue living two lives. We have simply got to stop being one thing around our Christian family and then totally different around those of the world. It amazes me how many Christians are more concerned about making impressions to the worldly, while being even embarrassed of their own brothers and sisters in the Lord.

Those who are living such dual identities are

only deceiving themselves. Those who are being
"Good with the Good" and "Bad with the Bad" are
not representing a distinction of the markings of
the blood of Christ.

In modern terms, God is saying, "Go mark those
who are grieving and angry about the sexual
immorality, abortion, child abuse, Satanism and
all other wickedness in the world today." God
wants to mark those who care about what is going
on. Mark those who are tired of the dishonor done
to God's Name. Mark those who seek His face for
the sins done around them.

Then He says to the men with axes, "Go after
him through the city and kill, do not let your eye
spare, nor have any pity. Utterly slay old and
young men, maidens and little children and
women, but do not come near anyone on whom is
the mark; and begin at My sanctuary."

Begin at God's sanctuary means begin at His
House—those buildings with crosses dotting the
landscape. They are sitting ducks if those inside
have not covered their sins with that cross of
Christ. Frightening! Peter knew this Scripture
well when he wrote, "It is time for the judgement
of God to begin with the family of God; and if it
begins with us, what will the outcome be for those
who do not obey the Gospel of God?"[4]

Beginning the judgement at God's sanctuary
must also indicate that there are those within
God's "family" who call themselves "Christians,"
but are not true children of God. We need to
examine ourselves to see if we are truly born again!
The next verse in Ezekiel states, "So they began
with the elders." How much more the elders of the
Church today must keep themselves blameless,
pure from the markings of the world.

The "mark" of God on our lives is the fruit of the Holy Spirit—our works, attitudes, decisions, reactions that serve as a testimony to others. "You will know them by their love," the Bible says and, "Judge them by their fruits."

We show our mark to the world, one mark or the other. If we are pleasers of the world instead of pleasers of God, those people around us will see that something is definitely wrong with us. We may be living according to the "lie" without realizing it!

The prayer we need to pray for each other is "Awake you who sleep, arise from the dead, and Christ will give you light!"[5] We as Christians need to ask God to open our eyes to deception so we can truly believe. God is exposing the idolaters in the Church who worship Him with their mouths, but do not do His Will.

My own belief is that we are nearing the end of God's commission to "Go mark" those who are truly His and His wrath is soon going to be poured out to destroy the idolaters, starting with those in the church. His love pleads with us to forsake sin, put it under the blood of Jesus, and cling to Him. A prayer of intercession today is for God to allow the Church to get itself in order before judgement comes. In verse eight, Ezekiel pleads for mercy on the house of Israel. His plea is similar to the picture Jeremiah gives us of Christ pleading for His Church.

God responds to Ezekiel that the Israelites are so wicked, they have convinced themselves that God "does not see" what they do. As if to illustrate how well He really does see, God says, "My eye will neither spare, nor will I have pity, but I will recompense their deeds on their own head."[6] Because God did not quickly execute judgement on them, they misjudged Him completely thinking He didn't even see their wickedness.

Peter tells us that God is patient with us—not so we can continue in sin for as long as we want—but because He gives the oppportunity to repent (2 Peter 3:9). God's boundless mercy and love is exhibited by His patience and longsuffering. We must not make the same mistake as Israel, assuming that because He waits, He doesn't see our sin.

The next chapter of Ezekiel, chapter ten, says God's glory then leaves the temple. We can expect the Glory of God to leave us if we do not follow the Lord. We can expect to revel in God's glory if we forsake all to follow Him.

I talk to many young people who attend heavy metal rock concerts and chant blasphemous sayings. "We spit at Calvary," they yell. They sing the words to songs such as, "Shout at the Devil," and "God Bless the Children of the Beast." Yet, they tell me that they've had experiences with God at church. I ask them, "What is it about the concerts that interests you?" They generally answer, "It's the power, the electricity of it all."

The power and the electricity. But God has all the power and electricity of the universe, so why aren't they attracted to church? Why are these young people who have been raised in church looking elsewhere for power and electricity? Where are all the miracles today like those recorded in the Book of Acts? Jesus said we would do greater things than Him, not fewer and smaller.

I know the answer—it takes personal consecration and commitment, daily dying to self, in every area of our lives. Before God will anoint us with

His power, we have to believe with our hearts. Belief in the world leads to consecration to the world. Belief in the Lord leads to consecration to the Lord.

For us to capture the young, to have the anointing of God, to be spared from judgement, we must be marked by God. We must be grieved in our hearts at the evil in the world today and ready to take a stand for righteousness. "Narrow is the gate that leads to life and wide is the gate that leads to death and destruction."[7]

NOTES:

[1] Prov. 1:7
[2] Prov. 8:13
[3] 2 Peter 3:9
[4] 1 Peter 4:17
[5] Eph. 5:14
[6] Ezk. 9:10
[7] Matthew 7:13-14

Part II
THE WILDERNESS JOURNEY

"And you shall remember that the Lord your God led you all the way these forty years in the wilderness, to humble you and test you, to know what was in your heart, whether you would keep His commandments or not.

"So He humbled you, allowed you to hunger, and fed you with manna which you did not know nor did your fathers know, that He might make you know that man shall not live by bread alone; but man lives by every word that proceeds from the mouth of the Lord.

"Your garments did not wear out on you, nor did your foot swell these forty years.

"So you should know in your heart that as a man chastens his son, so the Lord your God chastens you.

"Therefore you shall keep the commandments of the Lord your God, to walk in His ways and to fear Him.

Deuteronomy 8:2-6

7.

GETTING EGYPT OUT OF THE HEART

We can love the Lord and we can be filled with His Holy Spirit. We can aspire to serve Him in newness of life each and every day. Yet, we can still prevent the Lord from severing those things which hold us back from a total commitment to Him. Yes, we can be just like the children of Israel whom God delivered out of Egypt. Though they *were* delivered from Egypt, the children of Israel continued to yearn for the life which they had left behind. They continued to look back and long for the things of this world, rather than look forward to those great and precious promises of God. Yes, we can be, and often *are* just like the children of Israel in this respect. Lesson Learned: We can be delivered from the world physically and spiritually. However, that does not necessarily mean that we have been delivered from the *love* of this world spiritually speaking!

When the Red Sea thundered shut behind the children of Israel, there was no returning to Egypt. In their *hearts* however, Israel had yet to cross the Red Sea. The same is true in the world of evangelism today. We can take a kid off the streets and we can change his environment. Yet, the "streets" may still be in that young man's heart. We can even become a "Christian". Yet, if we refuse to deal with the sins in our own hearts, we will continue to live like we are still in the world! Instead of *hiding* behind the cross in this way, we should rather seek to be hidden in Christ that we might *truly* depart from the land of "Egypt".

If we have not properly dealt with the love of this world, then we will become slaves to our materialistic lusts rather than bond slaves to a righteous God. The church today has raised up many materialistic gods in their hearts, and thus has come to place an undue burden for the "work" of the ministry upon the *leaders* of the church. This is not the will of God, nor the order that God has ordained for His church. Ephesians 4:11-12 states the "work" of the ministry is a unique privilege of the *Body of Christ*. Yet, we exalt the elders of the 5-fold Ministries as "gods" expecting *them* to fulfill our God-ordained ministry while we go skipping off in pursuit of our own materialistic lusts.

Because of this ignorance of God's order, we no longer have a Body of Christ which is working together to fulfill it's evangelistic call. We are busy about our *own* business rather than our Father's business. We expect the *leaders* to carry the load instead of being faithful to the responsibilities which God has given to us. We look to fulfill our *own* selfish "needs" rather than being cognizant of the true needs around us. And when our leaders fall short in our own eyes, we get upset. We get upset with them and with God when we should really be pointing the finger at ourselves.

We cannot place our confidence in man. We

cannot place our confidence in our pastor or any other elder. Our confidence must be in *the Lord* and in His ability to speak through the leaders which He has chosen. And we must be *submitted* to God's order of authority even though we don't agree with certain decisions that are made, or certain actions that are undertaken. We are *accountable* to those whom God sets over us whether we agree with them or not and be assured that God does honor His governmental authority. The authority figure in your life could be in error in some area of life; however, God will still honor that man's *position*, or office of authority.

It is important to understand the distinction which the Lord makes here. God honors the office and not the man himself. The church in America on the other hand, honors the man rather than his God-ordained office. Thus, when these men fall, or fall into sin, much of the church also falls away. Why? Because their eyes are on the man and not the office. The man is human. The office is divine. When we use the fall of some man or woman of God as an excuse to justify our own departure from the faith, we only deceive ourselves and show that our trust is in man and not God. When we stand before the Lord, we won't be able to point our fingers at anyone but ourselves. God will say, "I am not interested in what someone else did; I want to know what *you* did when I confronted you with that place of truth in your life—when I confronted you with that remnant of "Egypt" in your heart?"

We must realize that those who are in positions of authority in our lives are human beings and not infallible gods; we sin when we exalt their humanity to god-like levels. We sin when we walk

away from them when they *do* fall because we are
the ones who placed them on the pedestal in the
first place. Rather than walk away, we need to
respect God's anointed. We need to realize that
they are human beings like anyone else, and as
human beings, they also will sin and fail. Therefore, when they fall, let us extend the same love
and mercy of God to them as we would to *anyone*
in our family. Let's *forgive* and restore upon *true
repentance* and let's stay *knitted* together as a
Body of Christ.

If there is one thing that I am grateful for, it is
for the *freedom* which we enjoy in America. I am
grateful for the freedom we have in seeking and
worshipping God as His Holy Spirit leads. Yet, in
America we have a church that has become an
institution. We have a church that has become a
deity. We have raised up this deity to serve ourselves. Yet, in actuality, we have become slaves
to it. We have become slaves of an *operation*,
rather than freemen of a living Holy Spirit.

The church in America therefore, has a choice
to make. Will we commit our hearts to God, or will
we give our lives to an organization?

In Colossians 4:14, we read about a man named
Demas. Demas' name means "popular" and from
this passage we see that Demas walked in ministry
with the Apostle Paul. In 2 Tim. 4:10, we read
about "Mr. Popular" again. Here we see that
Demas forsook Paul and the ministry which was
entrusted to him. Why? The scripture states the
reason in a very powerful way: Demas *forsook* the
ministry *"Having loved this present world" more
than he loved the Lord His God. How many of us*
have seen people leave the ministry, or depart from
their faith as did Demas because they loved the

things of this world more than the things of God? There is a message of *consecration* in the Bible, and it is what we *do* with this particular message that determines whether we become a Demas or a Timothy, a *true* disciple of the Lord.

We have a god in America called the god of Apathy and Complacency. Apathy and Complacency is a by-product of a wealthy and materialistic society. In many ways, America is a fantasy world. We think that nothing "bad" will ever happen to us. We refuse to deal with the real issues of life—the sin that resides deep in our hearts. Yet in America, we think that we are somehow immune from all adversity. The truth is that we have raised up a *god of false peace* which has *lulled us to sleep* through our own apathy and complacency. America is *not* immune and *will* be judged for the sins which our complacency has fostered.

Again, we all have a choice to make and that choice can make the difference between an Orpah and a Ruth. Orpah and Ruth were daughters-in-law of a godly woman named Naomi. The husbands of these three woman died during their sojourn in the country of Moab.[1] Naomi gave her daughters-in-law the choice to return to their own land or to remain with her. Naomi even encouraged them to return to their mother's house for she could offer them *nothing*. Orpah and Ruth both expressed their love for Naomi in tears, both stating that they would follow her wherever she would go. Many of us have expressed that same desire to Jesus. Many of us have expressed that same sorrow at the thought of departing from Jesus in favor of returning to our past lives. However,is our "sorrow" a *Godly* sorrow after the manner of Ruth, or is it a *sorrow without repen-tance* after the manner of Orpah?

Wives, you have expressed these exact same sentiments to your husbands. Husbands, you have expressed these exact same sentiments to your wives. However, how many of us are truly *committed to that confession?* Are we sorry enough to repent and remain faithful to our spouses and to our God no matter what the situation, no matter what the trial and no matter what the circumstance?

Orpah and Ruth both vowed to remain faithful to Naomi. However, whose words showed the *fruits of true repentance?* Whose words reflected true Godly sorrow *unto* committed action? Orpah returned to her pagan gods... Ruth remained. Naomi's seed had fallen on good soil. Ruth revealed the depth of her commitment to Naomi's God through her faithful commitment to Naomi herself.[2]

The scripture states that Orpah actually began her journey with Naomi and Ruth.[3] However, whatever commitment she did possess was based entirely upon "obligation" and being "the right thing to do", for she soon turned back as she "counted the cost" of her actions. Many of us are walking with Jesus with this exact same heart attitude. Many also reveal this same superficial commitment when faced with a choice as was Orpah, a choice to hold fast to the things of God and count the cost or to turn away and save our lives.[4]

Walking with Jesus because it is simply the "right thing to do" however, does not constitute a genuine commitment. There have been many great moves of God in the past few years; however, it was only *after* these moves occured when people wanted to become involved with the harvest. If such zeal had a true depth of commitment, then these people would have worked to *produce* the Harvest instead of coming out later after the enemy was already defeated.[5] Such "commitment" lacks courage and it lacks conviction.

The prophet Daniel is a good example of a man of conviction. Daniel chose not to cease his daily worship of Jehovah even though he knew that he could be thrown into the Lion's Den. He didn't make this commitment simply because it was the right thing to do, he made this commitment out of the deep convictions of his heart to be pleasing to his righteous Holy Father, who *alone* is worthy to be praised. The truth is (just like with Jesus), he would rather risk his life than sever his times of intimate fellowship with the Lord. He was committed to his God no matter what the cost and *that* is true commitment! Orpah eventually chose to go back on her initial commitment to remain faithful and to accompany Naomi. How many of us do the exact same thing with the Lord? How many of us begin to walk with God and be faithful to His commandments in certain areas of our lives and then turn away for the world? How many of us come to act like an Orpah at certain times in our lives, rather than a Ruth.

One of the greatest men of faith in the Bible is Abraham. Abraham was born "Abram". Abram was a wealthy and popular man from Ur. God brought Abram to a place of decision at one point in his life. God said to Abram, "I want you to leave your land and go to a land which I have prepared for you, a land where you will become the father of many nations". Abram obeyed God and went by faith not knowing where he was going. In doing so, Abram became "Abraham", the "Father of a Multitude" and the friend of God!

When we become christians, we also need to "go in faith", and become friends of God. We also need to come to that place of decision and choose God's path for our life rather than our own. No one can promise us that we *won't* face struggles and trials when we come to the Lord, however, if we remain faithful to God's will for our lives throughout all of those struggles and trials, we also will become the "Father of many blessings" in this life as well as the life to come.

The Word of God states that whatever we give up or lay down in this life will be given back a hundred fold in this life as well as everlasting life in the world to come.[6] Therefore, let us not be "weary in well-doing", and let us never turn back in our desire to draw even closer to the Lord.[7] God wants us to Cross the Jordan. He wants us to enter into this "Rest" that He has prepared for us in Jesus Christ. He wants us to enter into that place of promise so that we will reap His blessings no matter what our state and no matter what our circumstances in this life. Ruth found this place of rest and promise when she continued on and thus received a place of honor within the very lineage of the Messiah. Orpah, on the other hand, went back to her own gods to pursue her own way, and was never heard of again.

Now let's look at what our examples have in common! After Demas left Paul to seek the things of this world, we never hear about him again. Timothy, on the other hand, (as a true disciple of the Lord) cleaved to the Apostle Paul. It must not have been easy for Timothy at times, for the

Apostle Paul was so driven and intense in all that he said and did. However, because Timothy was truly committed to the things of God, his name went down in greatness.

Abram likewise made that commitment and continued on to become the Abraham of God. He received a name of greatness, and he became endeared, the "Father of a Multitude", the father of all those who became justified by *faith* in the God who *willingly* offered Himself up as a sacrifice for their sins.

Ruth has an entire book in the Bible written about her because she chose to cleave unto Naomi and the God which she represented. Joshua became the Captain of God's armies through his faithful commitment to minister to Moses, the man of God. *He went on to Cross the Jordan and possess the land,* thus entering into God's rest.[8]

The point in all of these examples is that those who choose to remain faithful to their commitment to seek the Lord with all of their heart will receive a name and place of honor forever in God's Kingdom.[9] On the other hand, those who turn away from their commitment to seek the Lord will disappear forever from the pages of history as did Korah.

Korah is an example of what happens when we rebel against God's governmental authority.[10] We become "swallowed up" in our own rebellious spirit and thus perish in our own rebellion and sin never to be heard from again.[11] However, let's put off such thoughts! Let's choose to go down in *greatness.* Let's *cleave* to Jesus even in the midst of our failures and overcome our sins by faith in His power within us to purge our wicked hearts. The scriptures state that a "righteous man" falls seven

times, yet always gets back up again.[12] Why?
Because that man is *committed*. He is committed
in his walk with the Lord and he doesn't turn back.
Thus, when he sins and falls he cleaves to Jesus
by faith. He cleaves to Jesus by trusting Him for
the grace to repent and the power to walk
"righteously" in those areas which are a struggle
for him. *We* need to "rise up" and Cross the
Jordan (in Jesus) this way, that we also might
enter into His promised "rest" in our own lives!

Between Egypt and the promised land was the
wilderness. The wilderness was intended to drive
Egypt out of their hearts, so that the faith of God
could truly reign in their lives. God removed Israel
physically from Egypt, but then He had to work to
remove them *spiritually* from the lusts of this
world. In the same way, it is easy to *physically*
remove ourselves from the actual outward acts of
sin. However, it is an entirely different matter to
get "Egypt" out of our *hearts!* Yes, we can physically stop taking drugs. We can physically cease
our prostitution, our lying and our rebellion. Yet,
can we spiritually "stop" our desire to do these
things in our heart? **Only God can deal with the
heart**. Yet, if we would but yield ourselves to Him
by faith *as* He deals with our hearts, we could
overcome even those "giants" in our lives! As with
Israel, the church also needs "the wilderness" in
order to have the lusts of this world removed from
their hearts. Therefore, let us yield ourselves to
Him. Let's *commit* our lives into His hands count-
ing Him faithful to finish that which He has begun
so beautifully in our hearts through Jesus!

The name of Demas means "popular". Maybe
his downfall was not being able to deal with Paul
being so recognized; maybe he couldn't deal with

the fact that Paul gave Timothy more attention. Perhaps he felt that he didn't get to preach enough or that he wasn't getting as much recognition as he wanted. Whatever the case, he decided to return to the pleasure of this world where the world will give "all the attention in the world".

In Acts Chapter 6, we find the appointment of Deacons. We need people appointed to take some of the duties to lift up the hands of our leaders. The men of God cannot neglect time in the Word of God or time *with* God. This means that others need to help carry the load. A prerequisite to being a man or woman of God is to have a servant's heart.

These seven men had to be of *good reputation, filled with the Spirit* and with *wisdom.* In this group were men such as Stephen and Philip. They were team players. They also knew their limits. Nicolas was also one of these seven men. He, therefore, fulfilled the necessary qualifications to hold the office of a deacon. Let's look at what happened to him and his followers in Revelation 2:6. God states there that he *hates* the deeds of the Nicolaitans and says in verse 15 that he also hates their *doctrine.* Why does God hate them? At some point, either Nicolas or one of his disciples could not let go of an area of his life—moral looseness. This group became known for its moral looseness and its sexual licentiousness.   God hates such liberality in His church for He would rather us be hot or cold. If we are "lukewarm" and walking in compromise of His Holy Command- ments, He will literally spew us out of His mouth.[13]

Instead of working as part of the team, Nicolaitans separated themselves and formed their own little group. Yes, other men like Peter,

Paul and the Apostle John formed other churches
which they themselves were responsible for discipling. However, all these churches were linked
together by common doctrine and by a common
love for the Lord and His Commandments.[14] The
Nicolaitans were different. These "Christians"
separated themselves from the rest of the churches by doctrine and by *action*.

The same is true within the church today. We
are all members of the Body of Christ who are
being discipled by different men in different churches. We are in a place of loving protection where
we are submitted to the leadership which God has
ordained, but we are also members of the Body of
Christ in total. This is God's plan for the
shepherding and discipleship of His people.[15]

Yet, there are those who are among us, who go
out from us never to return.[16] These go out from
us because they are seeking *other* "gods" to worship and serve.

Somewhere along the way, men such as Nicolas,
or one of his followers strayed from the covering
of God's governmental leadership. Demas left
because he wasn't popular enough and the
Nicolaitans wouldn't let go of the moral looseness
in their lives. They never wanted to surrender this
area of their lives to the Cross. God wanted to use
these people but they wouldn't let their flesh die.
The same is true with us when God brings us to
that place of decision in our lives. We don't *want*
the conviction. We don't *want* to seek repentance.
We want to return to our old "gods" and submit
ourselves to the bondage of our old sins. And often
times we *cheapen* God's grace by justifying our
involvement in sin, through the scripture that
says, "there is therefore now no condemnation to

those who are in Christ Jesus..."[17] If we would get a hold of a *real* Bible and read the second half of this verse (which has been deleted from many modern "versions"), we would see what Paul means by this statement.

"There is no condemnation" to those who walk according to the *Spirit*. There *is* however, condemnation to those who walk according to the *flesh*. Therefore, just like the Nicolaitans, there are those today who take the first half of Rom. 8:1 and go out from the Body of Christ to fashion their own abominable form of "Christianity." Instead of dealing with the conviction of God's Holy Spirit, they go back into the world where they can worship their own "gods" as they please while still maintaining a form of Christianity, a form of "godliness".[18] It is easier for them to succumb to their own lusts, than it is to *commit* themselves to seek the Lord so that such iniquity can be rooted out of their hearts!

Making that commitment however, will enable us to press on and to become victorious in the abominable areas of our lives. *Making* that commitment will enable us to Cross the Jordan and enter into God's promised "rest" in our relationship with Him!

Are you in some wilderness area in your life right now? If you are, then know that God is trying to deal with you. Know that God is trying to purge sin out of your heart so that He can replace it with faith and trust in Him. So what will you do with these words that you are reading? Will you deal with the issues at hand, or will you turn away from the "rest" and the blessing which God so earnestly desires for your life? Allow Jesus to get "Egypt" out of your heart. *Trust Him* to put the desire for true holiness in your life. As you allow the Lord to deal with your heart, He will take away all of the "dross" of Egypt and replace those voids with *Himself*. And the God of all comfort and peace shall indeed rule in your heart.[19]

Therefore, *become* a true disciple of the Lord as was Timothy. *Commit* to the way of holiness as did Ruth. Enter into "rest" as did Joshua and find the freedom in life that you have always desired to have . . . that *true* freedom which only is in the Lord Jesus Christ! Submit to God's governmental longing for your life and allow the ones whom God had appointed to "rule" over you in love to build you up in your most holy faith. *If you do these things, you will do well.* If you do these things, the Lord will remove "Egypt" out of your heart as well as out of your *actions*, and there will be no more restless striving with Him over the sins in your life! True peace and true blessing is walking with God, not fighting against Him every step of the way through the wilderness.

NOTES:

[1] Ruth 1:1-5
[2] Ruth 1:15-17
[3] Ruth 1:7
[4] In Luke 9:24, Jesus said "Whosoever will 'save' their lives will lose it, but whoever will lose their lives *for My sake* will save it.
[5] Judges 6:34-35; 8:1
[6] Matthew 19:27-30
[7] Galatians 6:7-10
[8] Joshua 24:15
[9] Rev. 2:17,26-28; 3:5,12
[10] Numbers 16

11 Prov. 21:16
12 Prov. 24:16
13 Rev. 3:16
14 Eph. 4:1-13
15 Eph. 4:7-32
16 1 John 2:19
17 Romans 8:1
18 2 Timothy 3:5
19 Col. 3:14-15; 2 Cor. 1:3-4

8.

THE DEVIL WANTS YOUR RIGHT EYE
(Your Vision of Hope)

In 1 Thessalonians 5:1-11, the Lord exhorts us not to "sleep", but to watch and be sober lest the Day of the Lord overtake us as a thief in the night. If we are faithful to prepare for His coming in this way, the Day of the Lord won't overtake us in total surprise. Through "watching", praying and going about the business of the Lord, we will remain sensitive to the Holy Spirit of God. Being sensitive to the Holy Spirit will enable us to see the changing of the seasons and we will know when we are in the "season" of His coming!

Until the Day of His Coming, Jesus Himself is the hope which the Lord has set before us. *His* hope was not looking to the intense suffering of the Cross. The joy which the Father had set before Him was to look beyond the Cross. Jesus looked beyond the Cross knowing that through His obedience to His Father's will, He would bring many sons into glory. In other words, Jesus' hope was that some day you and I would be reconciled and in right relationship with the Father through

our faith in *Him!* Jesus then, *is* our hope! Our
hope is found by looking *beyond* our circumstances, *beyond* our trials and frustrations and looking
unto Him.

We can have an *expectant* hope if we properly
discern the times and are aware of the season of
His coming. Noah was a man who heeded the
voice of God thus discerning the time of the Lord's
visitation. He preached repentance unto
righteousness and informed the people that judgement was coming. It would come through a flood
which would cover all of the earth. A few might
have been shaken up by his message but they
either procrastinated in their decision or ignored
Him completely. For forty or fifty years Noah
warned, "A flood is coming; repent." Soon one
hundred years passed and still no one took him
seriously. Was Noah lying? Was he insane? Of
course, not! After 120 years of bulding, he completed the ark and judgement came. The season
of the Lord's coming had arrived at last!

In each generation, preachers have been saying,
"Get ready; Jesus is coming soon." I believe that
this generation of preachers today is saying, "Get
ready for this *is* the generation of the Lord's literal,
physical return to earth." I also believe that we
really need to be encouraged and *heed* this message. We *need* to be encouraged that we might
fully embrace the Lord's exhortation to us in 1
Thessalonians 5:23. That is, that we might allow
Him to "sanctify us wholly" thus receiving *peace*
during these troubled times. There is peace in true
repentance before our God. There is joy and true
refreshing of His Holy Spirit when we prepare our
hearts to receive Him into every area of our lives.
Let's be encouraged then, and experience the true

freedom which is in Jesus Christ. When we experience that freedom, it is then that we can become truly accountable to God through humble submission to His will in every area of our lives!

The Lord wants us to take this expectant hope out into the ministry to which He has called us.[1] Matt. 28:18 states that all power in heaven and earth has been given to Jesus in order to accomplish this ministry. In Acts 4, we see what happens when we try to move in *the authority which God has granted us in the Name of Jesus.* The principalities and powers of this world, whether they be in the spirit or whether they be in the flesh, try to stop us. The devil hates the authority which we have been given in the Name of Jesus. Therefore, he does everything that he can to hinder and discourage us from talking about Jesus and making disciples of all nations. The devil does everything he can to negate the authority which we have in Jesus' Name. He does this by stealing the Word of God out of our hearts, and by killing our hope in Jesus.[2] He wants to destroy the vision which God has given us.[3]

The first half of Prov. 29:18 states that, "where there is no vision, the people perish. . .". If satan succeeds in destroying our hope in the coming of our Lord, and the vision God has given us, then he will have succeeded in disarming the Church and taking the "fight" out of our spirits. Indeed, how *can* we fight when we have allowed him to strip us of the authority which God has given us? We need to follow the example *which God has provided in Peter and the rest* of the apostles in Acts 4!

When confronted by the principalities and powers of this world, will we lay down our vision?

Will we give up the authority we have in Jesus' Name? Or will we stand *strong?* Will we pray and continue to be filled with God's Holy Spirit saying, "there is salvation in no other name (but Jesus) under heaven, and we cannot but speak of the things which we have seen and heard!?"[4] The devil knows that there is no salvation, no deliverance, no peace, no joy, nor victory outside of the Name of Jesus. He knows *that there is no power, nor any demonstration* of the presence of God's Holy Spirit to destroy his works, if he has succeeded in putting out our "right eye"—deceiving us into laying down the authority which we possess in the Name of Jesus.

Again, in Acts 4:20, Peter's response to the devil's deception is that, "we cannot but speak the things which we have seen and heard". In other words, not only are they sold-out, and *excited* about Jesus, but they are also *accountable* for what they have been given—**Grace** to see and to hear. This brings up a very important point; authority cannot be given without accountability. Authority goes hand-in-hand with God's purpose in this life. And that purpose is that we might successfully destroy the works of the devil by accomplishing the great commission which has been given us in Matt. 28:18-20. Remember, all power in heaven and earth has been given us in the **Name of Jesus** so we will accomplish this great task! Therefore, we are *accountable* for what God has given us. We are accountable for all that He has given us, the grace to see and to hear in His Name. Therefore, let us *not* be slack, nor afraid of speaking all that we have seen and heard concerning the Person of Jesus, the only true and living God!

There is no doubt that we are closer to the return of Jesus than we have ever been before. As we approach that day, more and more people are becoming offended at the Name of Jesus. We are seeing sharp divisions between the sheep and the goats, as well as the sheep and the *sheep*. "Judgement" which must first come upon the house of God, will draw a line within the church and then proceed out into the world.[5] This line is represented by the title of this book, "Who Will Cross The Jordan?" Who will leave their lives of sin and compromise behind and become fully committed in heart to the things of God (as was evidenced by the example of Ruth).

We are being challenged in these days to *"keep the fight alive"*. We are being challenged by the principalities and powers of this world, as well as by the Lord Himself. What will we do? Will the Church of Jesus Christ *answer* the call to consecration? We will if Jesus is *truly* our hope, our salvation and our deliverance. We will if we realize that *Jesus* (not ourselves) is the fight that lives within us.

In 1 Samuel 11, we see historical example of what the devil is trying to do to the Church today. It ought to make us *angry* with a righteous *anger!* It ought to make us furious that the devil would try to mutilate the Bride of Christ in the way we see in this chapter. Nahash means "serpent" and thus becomes a type of the devil in 1 Samuel 11. The men of Jabesh fear Nahash and desire to make a covenant with him. A covenant whereby they can peacefully co-exist with him in servitude *to* him. Well, God shows us that this is not possible. God shows us what satan really wants to do to the Bride of Christ. We see that there is *no* covenant-making with the devil. Satan is only satisfied with our total humiliation, total disgrace and our total destruction!

1 Samuel 11:2 states that satan wants to "put out our right eye" that he might bring a reproach and thus bring disgrace upon the people of God. The heart attitude here is the same as what the Philistines did to Samson when they put out *both* of his eyes, bound him in chains, mocked him and then made sport with him before *all of the people.*[6] Satan wants to do the same thing to each and every one of us today! Do you see why we should be furious in the Name of Jesus at his demeaning tactics? The devil wants our "right eye" that he might totally *demean* God's chosen people. He wants to totally disarm the Church in our efforts to accomplish our commission to destroy his works on this earth!

What is so significant about the "right eye"? In ancient days, a soldier would take up his shield (just as we take up our "shield of faith" in the Spirit!) in his left hand. He took up his sword in his right hand. As the attack loomed closer, the soldier would look around the shield with his *right* eye in order to gauge the enemy's whereabouts and to know where to strike him. Without his right eye then, the soldier would be totally crippled in his attempt to ward off and conquer the enemy.

The same is true for us today in the realm of the spirit. If we allow satan to "put out our right eye", we will be crippled in our attempts to attack and destroy his works amongst the children of men! The men of Jabesh-Gilead succumbed to the enemy's *discouraging threats* instead of "encouraging themselves in the Lord" and trusting God to deliver them. Through the sin of dis-

couragement, the men of Jabesh lost all desire to
fight. If it had not been for God's saving grace in
the Person of His anointed king, King Saul, the
men of Jabesh-Gilead would have *lost* their right
eye forever! Therefore, they would have lost their
ability to contend with the enemy in all future
occurences.

God has saved us by His grace through His
anointed king, **Jesus**. In Jesus, we have no reason
to ever become discouraged for "His is the
Kingdom and the Power, and the Glory, forever
and ever"! We have *all power* in the Name of Jesus
to destroy the works of the enemy. The men of
Jabesh-Gilead were, no doubt, strong warriors.
However, they were dry in their hearts and ex-
tremely lax in their trust in the Lord.[7] This
lukewarm relationship with God coupled with the
sin of unbelief caused these men to become *discouraged* and thus they temporarily lost their
spiritual "right eye of might". If they had been
given no savior, they would have lost their *physical*
right eye as well.

Again, the same is true with us today concerning *spiritual* warfare. When, through a lukewarm
relationship with God, we lose our joy, our hope
and His vision for our lives, we also lose our
strength and our will to resist the devil in all of his
works! We are *content* as were the complacent
men of Jabesh-Gilead, to let the enemy walk right
in and totally demean us, to totally destroy our
will and our ability to fight against his devices.
Let's get back our "right eye". Let's get back our
will to fight in Jesus' Name and fight the good fight
of *faith!* Let's continue to run the race *until* we
obtain that ultimate prize in Christ Jesus!
Rebuke discouragement in the Name of Jesus and

praise Him for the victory that has *already* been won!

The "Savior" of 1 Samuel 11:3 came in the Person of Saul. Today we have Jesus and a much better covenant. When it seems like all odds are against us and we need help, we can call on Jesus to help us and *Jesus never fails!* We are joint-heirs with Him and He is seated at the right hand of the Father saying, "I will move on your behalf". We have got to perceive in our spirit that when we cry out in the Name of Jesus, we *know* that He hears us and that He *is* moving on our behalf.[8] He is there for us no matter what the circumstances are. We never have to run scared. When we stand firm in Jesus with perfect hearts towards His will and purpose for our lives, the devil doesn't stand a chance. Again, **Jesus is the "right eye" of our fight. Jesus is the "right eye" of our righteousness and Jesus is our vision of hope.** If we take Jesus *out* of our lives, our actions, and our conversation, we have taken the fight right out of our lives! I believe that God wants to renew a right spirit within His Church today, a spirit that will take up His Cross and fight that good fight of faith until He comes again!

God's kingdom is not only coming, but it is here now as well.[9] Do you remember what Jesus said in Luke 17:21? He said that the Kingdom is *within* us. In other words, God's presence is in our hearts, and wherever *He* dwells, there dwells His kingdom, as well. Therefore, we don't have to wait until He *physically* comes to establish His Kingdom here on earth. We can *begin* to show forth His presence right here and now. As *our* hearts are prepared for the establishment of His Kingdom, let us also seek to prepare *other* hearts for His coming.

Colossians 1:12 teaches that God has *qualified* us to be a partaker of His inheritance. He has qualified us in Jesus to take this inheritance and offer it to a sick world through the Gospel, that the world might be healed: spirit, soul and body. Part of our inheritance in carrying out this commission is to walk in *His* victory, in *His* power and in *His* "right eye" of faith, fight and hope. Only through Jesus can we fight the good fight of faith as His joy (joy in the inheritance of our Lord) becomes our strength. To fight the battles of this life in our own strength is to invite discouragement and eventual failure and defeat.

2 Corinthians 10:3-5 states that the weapons of our warfare are *not* carnal. They have absolutely nothing to do with our own strengths and abilities. Rather, they are mighty through *God* to the pulling down of strongholds. Thus, the weapons of our warfare have *everything* to do with **Jesus.** Through Jesus we can cast down every sin, ungodly instruction, *everything* that exalts itself against the knowledge of God. If we are double-minded and doubt the power of God, let's not think that we will be able to overcome anything in His Name.[10] However, if we exalt *Jesus, His* promises, and His Words, then we become a partaker of *His* Kingdom, overcoming all that opposes His will and purpose in our lives. In this specific way, do we bring every thought captive to the obedience of Christ!

Therefore, when you hear the lies that say, "you have no fight in you and you will not be able to go another day", bring that thought into the obedience of Christ. **Exalt Jesus.** Exalt His Word which says that we have an inheritance of faith, victory and power in Him. Exalt His Word which states that we *are* the righteousness of God in Him. Bring down *every* thought to the obedience of Christ that comes against your mind and is contrary to God's promise, vision and hope for your life. If you feel yourself beginning to doubt God and losing trust in Him, in a certain situation, rebuke fear in the Name of Jesus.[11] Take that thought captive, putting it to death in His Name. We can trust the Lord implicitly because He is not a "man" that He should lie!

If we lose our hope and vision of God's promise, then we are giving up His Kingdom and giving place to a lie. It is the lie of this world that says that there is no hope, no peace nor joy. We cannot give place to the world or any of its lies. Cast down these lies in the Name of Jesus and renew your mind in Him. *Obey* the Word of God and overcome all of the devices of the enemy that would rob you of your joy, as you destroy his works.

We lose our joy when we disobey the first and greatest command of God, "to love Him with all of our heart, with all of our soul, and with all of our might." We lose our joy when we give place to the thoughts of this world by spending more time with the things of this world than with the Lord Himself.[12] Are we spending time with God, giving Him our minds, or are we giving our minds over to the television, the music and the lusts of this world? When we do the latter, we lose our joy and thus, we lose our strength in the Lord (just like Sampson). We are no longer being *spiritually* discerning. Rather, we are being naturally and carnally-minded and this is when the devil comes to possess our right eye.

When this happens, it is time to grab hold of the

Cross. It is time to *repent*, to grab hold of Jesus, our Rock! *He* is the right eye of our faith. He is our righteousness and thus will renew our minds, our joy and our *strength* if we repent (as also did Sampson- Judges 16:22-30). We must commit to giving place only to Jesus! We must commit to obeying only *Him* lest we be overcome by the lusts of this world.

Let's put on the mind of Christ. When the devil comes against us, let's walk in our authority as joint-heirs with Christ. Let's perceive the character of the One who died for us and know not only His judgement, but also His *love*. When we repent we must see ouselves as *He* sees us; then we will begin to walk in His victory.[13]

We must destroy those little seeds of sin in our lives, that can grow up and totally separate us from the presence of the Lord. Matthew 21:44 speaks of Jesus as *The Rock*. We can either fall upon the Rock and find repentance and restoration in Him or we can continue in our sin; thus, we invite God's judgement to fall upon us (grinding us to powder-Prov. 27:22). If we take those little sins and crucify them now, we will escape the judgement that is to come. If however, we are unwilling to repent, we will be crushed by the very things which we refuse to surrender. We can choose life willingly and have joy and peace in Jesus, today. Or, we can walk straight into a miserable wilderness, which we may never leave. Which will it be? The Lord is desiring to set us back upon a **road of vision and hope** that we might fight that good fight of faith in Him. Therefore, let's cast down that sin of unbelief which so *easily* besets us! Let's take every thought captive to the obedience of Christ. Don't let the devil have *your right eye—your vision of hope in Jesus*, who sits at the right hand of the Father as your right *eye of righteousness!*

NOTES:

1 Matt. 28:18-20
2 Matt. 13:1-22
3 John 10:10
4 Acts 4:11-12;4:20
5 1 Pet. 4:17
6 Judges 16:21-25
7 Jabesh means dry.
8 Ps. 34:15
9 Matt. 6:10
10 James 1:5-8
11 2 Tim. 1:7
12 2 Tim. 2:4
13 Phil. 3:5-8

9.

OASIS FOR THE WEARY TRAVELER

What really matters to the people of God today? What is it that we truly pursue in life? Think about it. Do we pursue that vast array of pleasures which has become a hallmark of our hedonistic society, or do we pursue the knowledge of God with all diligence and intensity? Are we just "Christians", or are we true disciples of the Lord? There *are* those who stumble and fall; however, their whole motivation is to keep on cleaving to Jesus. They are *determined* to cling to Jesus that the sins in their lives might fall away into oblivion. If we want to find that place of complete victory, we must seek the Lord in this way with all diligence and intensity.

What is it if we pursue the things of the world and even **gain** those things, yet in the process, we end up losing our own soul? We plan and we toil to "get". However, are our plans and possessions of any lasting value?

In James chapter five, we read about the "rich" and think that this address doesn't pertain to us. Yet in America, even the "impoverished" are rich compared to many other people in the world. We are rich not only in material things, but we are

blessed also in spiritual things. A great spiritual
feast has been set before us here in America since
its very inception as an independent republic. Yet,
what have we done with such knowledge?

We are often quick to go deeper into debt that
we might partake of the luxuries and pleasures of
this world. Yet when it comes to the House of the
Lord, and spreading the Gospel through our time,
talents, and finances, we are just as quick to say,
"We don't *have* enough. . ." We don't have enough
time, nor talent, nor money. Yet, we do have
enough time to enjoy that new car, new health club
membership, etc. We *do* have enough talent to
embark upon our own self-serving projects. Yes,
we even have enough money to finance our own
hobbies and extracurricular activities. I would
say that we need to take a look at our priorities in
life.

In James 5:4, we see the cry of the laborers
coming before the Lord as they are hard at work
out in the fields. Who are these laborers? Pastors,
teachers, evangelists, apostles, prophets, mis-
sionaries and whoever else has "laid down their
life" for the Gospel's sake. These are the laborers
of James 5:4. These are they who have sur-
rendered their lives to the Lord of Hosts and who
have heeded His calling on their lives. These are
those who labor among you, planting spiritual
blessings in your hearts that you might go out and
do the work of the ministry.[1]

Yet, the people of God have forsaken their calling and have placed the entire burden of the "work
of the ministry" on the shoulders of the eldership.
Thus the cries of these laborers are coming before
the Lord of the Harvest because *they* are in lack
while *we* are in plenty, pursuing the things of this

world, rather than the things of God![2] God is looking for people who will simply make themselves available for His use. He is looking for people who are *willing* to heed His call. Let's take our responsibilities concerning the Gospel *seriously.* Let's *rethink* our priorities in this life. Even if you think that you have absolutely nothing to give, you do have something to give. You can give your *prayers* for those who are willing to do the work of the ministry each and every day. And *prayer* is no light matter! There is a vast shortage of it within the Church today.

Proverbs 27:7 states that the "*full* soul loathes the honey comb", but "to a *hungry* soul, every bitter thing is sweet." When you think that you can do nothing to help, or that you have nothing to give, please realize that you do have something to offer. You can offer God your *hunger*. Make yourself available to Him and *pray* for God's hunger in your life, and He will fill your hungry soul with the "bitter-sweet" work of His ministry. As 2 Chronicles 16:9 says, "the eyes of the Lord run to and fro throughout the whole earth, to show Himself *strong* on behalf of them whose heart is perfect toward Him"!

There is so much that we can all do if we would but only pray for this "hungry heart" which the Lord speaks of. We *can* bring Jesus to those who have need of Him. The Lord simply desires our *faithfulness* to bring His life to those who are hungry, thirsty, and dying. The world *needs* to see the Word of God living in us and being expressed through us in the form of His all-encompassing love. We need to reach out to this world with the love of the Lord Jesus Christ not only with words, but with *actions* as well![3] Again, you may not think that you have what it takes to help others and to effectively share the Gospel, but you do. You have the two most important elements: your hunger and your *availability*. God simply desires you to make yourself available to Him. Make yourself available and allow Him to use the hunger within your heart to glorify His Name! Nothing is more precious to God than a *willing* vessel through which He can do great exploits! If we are faithful to Him in this, He will show Himself faithful to us.

As a vessel of the Lord, we often go through "dry times" when it is easy to lose our vision and our hope through the enemy's lies and discouraging tactics. Discouragement even makes it hard for us to *trust* in God. These are times when we feel as if there is nothing left within us to give and thus feel like giving up! We need to get past this point, so that the storms and temptations of this life will not move us off of that foundation which is in Christ Jesus. When we are in physical, spiritual or emotional distress, we need to come back to the word of God, and *stand* in absolute faith upon it! As a vessel of the Lord, we *will* experience many temptations in this life. And when these temptations come, we need to cast them down in the Name of Jesus and say, "No, the *Word* says . . . ." The difference between a Christian and a true disciple of the Lord is their knowledge and *application* of the Word of God in their life! God's commission is not to call people to salvation only but it is to make *disciples!*

The power and victory of Jesus evidenced in and through our life does not come from just knowing *about* God (knowledge). It comes from walking in *intimacy* with Him each and every day (relationship). In this place of knowledge and relationship, the power of God that raised Jesus from the dead can meet us in our time of need and keep us faithful in the things of God whenever trials and temptations come our way. Such a personal relationship with a *Living* God brings joy to our lives in times of mourning and brings freedom of thought in times of attack when the devil would seek to oppress our minds with all manner of lies. This is the legacy of a true disciple, a true vessel of the Lord; it is part of our *inheritance* in Jesus, and we can have this peace, this "rest" right here and right now—if we would but abide in Him as we go about His business each and every day.[5]

In John 12:12-19, we read about Jesus riding into Jerusalem on a donkey. As He rode into the city, the people of Jerusalem threw down *Palm Branches* in His path and stood on either side waving these palm branches before Him. This was prophetic action. They were not only fulfilling scripture and hailing the return of the King of Kings to His city,[6] but they were also hailing Him as their "Oasis in the desert".

Palm trees grow in fertile areas in the midst of the desert; these fertile areas are fed by underground springs and are called *oasis.* When you find a palm tree in the desert therefore, you have found an oasis. And if you have found an oasis, you have most certainly found *water.* The palm tree itself provides two things. It provides *shade* from a hot and burning sun, and it provides a nutritious food in the *dates* which it produces. The date palm also represented the place of *judgeship* in the scriptures. In fact, the sole reason why Jesus rode into Jerusalem on a donkey was because it was also a symbol of

judgeship and thus Jesus becomes the perfect
fulfillment of all of the Holy scriptures, no matter
how small the detail!

So to the weary traveler, the palm tree represented a place where he could find *shade* from the
hot sun. It represented a place of rest where He
could refresh and strengthen himself with food
and water. In a sense, it was a place where his
weariness was judged. And along with judgement,
came refreshment and healing.

When those people gathered together to usher
Jesus into the City with the waving of the palm
trees, did they really understand what they were
doing? Did they truly perceive the symbolic ges-
tures of their actions? Does the Church today
understand the symbolism of the palm tree? How
about you? Is there a divine "Palm Tree" in your
life?

Jesus Himself *is* our "palm tree". He is the
living fulfillment of judgeship in our lives. He is
the palm tree for all that makes us weary as we go
through this life. Jesus is the living fulfillment of
that *spiritual* shade, that *spiritual* drink and that
spiritual food which sustains and strenghtens us
in a dry and thirsty land.[7] Jesus didn't just die
on the cross for our sins. He came to give us rest
in the midst of our labor and travail.[8] Jesus came
to give us life, and life more abundantly! He
poured out *His* life for a dry and thirsty world and
He was raised from the dead that our mourning
might be turned into dancing and that our defeat
might be turned into *victory*.

The key to all of this is *discipleship*. This word
probably best describes that personal and intimate relationship which the Lord is so anxious
to enjoy with each and every one that will come to

Him with a broken and contrite heart. The
Church can no longer be spectators in a lost and
dying world. The Church can no longer afford to
merely "profess" their Christianity. *We need
relationship.* We need a heart of true discipleship
in our lives.

Now then, allow me to present the same challenge to you as I continually present to myself.
What kind of Christian are you? There are really
only two kinds. There is one who is *grieved* of
spirit when convicted of his sin. This disciple runs
to Jesus *upon* that conviction and pleads for mercy
and forgiveness, seeking the grace of God to depart
from that sin forever and ever. The other Christian does not perceive the conviction of the Holy
Spirit thus remaining content with his or her own
ways. This one *hardens* his heart toward the Lord
in this way and does not enter into God's calling
of *true* discipleship!

Do you see the difference? A true disciple of the
Lord is grieved of his sin and runs to God while
the other justifies *himself* saying, "well, we are all
just human and God can't expect us to be perfect
anyway. Besides, God doesn't really mean it when
He says . . . ." This is the person that begins to
point the finger and to preach about what should
be done in the church instead of concentrating on
what should be done in his or her own life, first!

One evidence of this type of attitude is in the
area of divorce. We wonder why the Body of Christ
possesses a divorce rate almost as high as the
world, itself. Discipleship is *relationship!* Marriage is *relationship.* The "mystery" of the
Kingdom is right relationship with God, *right*
relationship between the Groom and the Bride,
right relationship between Christ and the Church.

Therefore, if we refuse to deal with our own sins and continually point the finger as if the problem lies outside of our own "selves", then we cannot *but* separate ourselves from our own spouses. And *if we divorce ourselves so easily from each other, what are we doing to our relationship with God?*9, 10

This "escapist" attitude is all too prevalent within the Church. If we don't like the Pastor's message, we go to another church. If we don't like the conviction which we get in one place, we run somewhere else. We escape; we run from our own selfish sins so much that we end up not being accountable to anyone, let alone He that is supposed to be the Lord of our lives. We don't stay submitted *anywhere* long enough for our sins to be exposed and dealt with. God is looking for a *commitment* within the Body of Christ today—a commitment to allow Him to deal with our sins so that the basic building block of the Church, the *Family*, will be healed and restored. This will happen *only* when the Body of Christ commits to becoming submitted to God's authority in their lives. Submission to *God's* authority brings about that *true* freedom which is in Christ, not the "escapist" type mentality which comes as a result of asserting our *own* authority.

Luke 19:41-44 shows Jesus to be weeping over the state of Jerusalem. I am convinced that Jesus is weeping over the condition of His church in this exact same way. He weeps over the division within His church. He weeps over the compromise that He sees in our lives. He weeps over the strongholds of sin which we allow to remain in our hearts, thus separating ourselves from Him. Jesus weeps over the needs which are not being

met. He weeps over the weary travelers who are
struggling through the wilderness.

Jesus weeps and yet, according to His ines-
timable love, His ears are always open to our cry.[11]
As we struggle and toil in frustration through a
dry and thirsty land, the Lord is saying, "I will
never leave or forsake you. Your raiment will not
wax old and your foot will not swell.[12] Keep looking; keep seeking my face and you will find the
oasis which you are looking for in Me. When you
find My shade and My comfort, I will move through
you to comfort the hurting of this world. When
you drink of My living water and eat of My meat,
I will move through you to quench the hunger and
thirst of a lost and dying world!"

We tend to think that hunger is a problem
unique to third world countries. Yet, there is a
famine in the church for the Word of God like never
before. We can satisfy the longing of the physical
body from meal to meal, but we ourselves, *cannot*
satisfy the longing within our souls. Only the
palm tree of Christ taking deep root within our
hearts can satisfy such a deep spiritual need.
Jesus is asking us all to drink of His life. If we are
weary travelers in our walk with Him, He is asking
us to dig down and find that Living Water which
is in Him.[13]

He is asking us to cleave to *Him*, to abide *in* Him,
that we might know that He is for us and not
against us, that we might know that He has a
future of *good* planned for us and not of evil! Once
we discipline ourselves and submit to Him in this
way, He will give us all that we need to overcome
the "giants" of this life.

What is it that *you* have need of? The palm tree
is symbolic of so much? Aside from what we have

already discussed, the palm tree is a figure of
flourishing in righteousness.[14] In Rev.7:9 and
John 12:13, the palm boughs become a symbol of
the ultimate victory of Jesus as King of Kings and
Lord of Lords. The palm tree is a figure of beauty
in the Song of Solomon. The palm tree is also
symbolic of patience, strength and prosperity.
The *leaves* of the palms are used in the building
of roofs, fences and houses. Thus, the palm tree
becomes the primary element in the construction
of the desert dwelling place, the abiding place of
refuge in the midst of the wilderness!

Jesus is our dwelling place! He is our abode in
the wilderness! Jesus Himself, is our "palm tree"
who provides everything we need to fulfill the
longing of our souls. Whatever the longing of your
soul may be, *He* is the complete satisfaction and
fulfillment of that longing! Jesus said that His
"meat" was to do the will of the Father who sent
Him.[15] In other words, His *complete satisfaction*
in life was to do what pleased the Father and *that*
is what brought Him complete fulfillment! *We*
should covet that same heart attitude. We also
should find fulfillment and satisfaction only in
what pleases our loving Father. There is nothing
like knowing you have heard your Father's voice
and *knowing* that you have obeyed and honored
Him![16]

We *all* have embarked upon a journey in this
life, but the question is to where? Are we journeying *up* the path of righteousness, or are we journeying *down* the path of sin and unbelief? Are we
journeying down the path of rebellion and self?
Those who are ascending the path of righteousness are *guaranteed* oases in the midst of their
deserts. Those who forsake this path, however,

"will remain in the congregation of the dead."[17] The key rests within the pursuits and desires of our own hearts. Is our whole heart's desire to find the knowledge of God and to continually seek to grow in right-relationship with Him? Or is the desire of our heart simply to pursue the things which this world has to offer? Yes, it is our *heart* that will determine our path in this life as well as our fate in the life beyond!

Now the path of righteousness includes a vision of hope. This hope is an eternity of intimate fellowship with the One who gave Himself for our sins. Until this hope is finally realized, the Lord is challenging us not to lose sight of His coming, as we journey through this life. "Holding on" to this hope which has been set before us will serve to continually *encourage* us as we journey through this life, sharing *His* life with those around us. In the midst of our desert, the Lord is challenging us, *pleading* with us to take and eat of the comfort and nourishment which is found only in Jesus. *He* is our palm tree when we become weary travelers in this life. *He* is our rest and *He* is our refreshing during our time of need. Therefore, come to Jesus. He is the oasis for the weary traveler!

"Come to Me, all you who labor and are heavy laden, and I will give you rest.

Take My yoke upon you and learn from Me, for I am gentle and lowly in heart, and you will find rest for your souls.

For My yoke is easy and My burden is light."

Matt. 11:28-30

DON'T GIVE UP

Do you feel your light has grown dim?
Search out your heart, reach down from within,
Do you find Him?
It is He, you should see, if you believe.

CHORUS:
Don't give up, He's not through with you
Don't give up, know that His love, His love is
true,
The storms you face, my Jesus will see you
through,
So don't give up.

Be strong in the power of His might,
Stand on your feet,
Walk by faith, not by sight,
Fight that good fight,
We can win, conquer sin,
When we reign, reign with Him.

CHORUS:
Don't give up, He's not through with you,
Don't give up, know that His love, His love is
    true,
The storms you face, my Jesus will see you
    through,
So don't, don't give up.

NOTES:

[1] Ephesians 4:11-13
[2] Of *our* time, talents and finances
[3] James 2:14-26
[4] Matthew 28:19-20
[5] John 15
[6] Zech. 9:9
[7] 1 Cor. 10:1-4
[8] Matthew 11:28-30
[9] Through our own sins, not the other person's
[10] Mal. 2:10-17
[11] Psalm 34:19
[12] Deu. 8:1-5
[13] John 7:37-40
[14] Psalm 92:12
[15] John 4:34
[16] Matthew 25:23
[17] Prov. 21:16

10.

SEVEN OPPOSITIONS OF THE ENEMY

When we make the quality decision to go on with God, certain trials and distractions are going to challenge our commitment. These oppositions of the enemy are meant to discourage us from achieving the object of our faith, intimacy with our Lord Jesus Christ. Be aware of the enemy's tactics so he won't catch you off guard. When you become discouraged you are open to falling into deception which can lead to compromise. If we are discouraged and doubt God's perfect plan and vision for our lives, we are then in a state of unbelief. We're saying in essence, "God, I don't believe You will come through." When we fall for this lie of the devil, we can fall into compromise. Compromise is straying from the straight and narrow path of righteousness; it is sin which separates us from God and prevents us from going forward in our relationship with Him. Beware of the enemy's opposition for his whole goal is to pull you away from your commitment to the Lord.

Today we look at the Body of Christ and see the hurts, the needs, and the frustrations. In one sense we're giving God praise with our lips, but we're living in defeat. We're concerned for the dying world, but we need a persevering spirit to keep on fighting. We get distraught and discouraged at times. We see the sins sweeping across the Body of Christ and we wonder if there's any escape. We see the enemy coming against our minds and telling us lies. We cry, "God, am I ever going to get free from this?" Yes, you can and we will see how through the book of Nehemiah. We will take a look at the seven threats and oppositions that came against Nehemiah when he determined to seek the well-being of God's people.

Nehemiah wept for Jerusalem, just as we should weep for the Body of Christ, today.[1] Before an outpouring of the Holy Spirit can come, there must first be weeping before God for our sins and true repentance. There must be true comprehension of the Cross. Then the outpouring that we see in Acts chapter two, will come. After the outpouring, then comes the equipping to go forth in power. Through Jesus Christ, God has given us the opportunity to leave the world, defeat and captivity behind!

In the book of Ezra, God opened the door for Israel to return to Jerusalem and rebuild the Temple. Out of a population of two to three million people, only fifty thousand were willing to answer God's call and leave behind the Babylonian society with all of its comforts. It was a nine hundred mile journey from Babylon to Jerusalem and when they arrived, they found a city and a Temple that had been in ruins and they had much rebuilding to do![2] The walls of Jerusalem represented protection for Israel. When the walls were rebuilt they would protect the people from the enemy's attacks.

In like manner, the walls of the church, need to be rebuilt and when completed, these walls will protect us from satan's attacks. We need to build the walls in our relationship with God and with each other. Many people grow weary, and then apathetic and complacent, just like the children of Israel. But if we neglect the building of the walls, we will be vulnerable to the enemy's attacks.

Nehemiah saw what had happened to God's people. He wept over the apathy, complacency and compromise. For this reason, we see Nehemiah praying and fasting for a people who were letting down their guard. Can we fast and pray and stand in the gap for the Body of Christ today? Can we set aside our own desires in order to bring restoration to the Church? Our brothers and sisters are hurt and struggling in their relationship with God and others. We need to be a part of rebuilding their lives. We are so indulgent. We want to *get*, but are we willing to *give*? We say, "When do we get to rest?" We don't rest until the world has had its last chance and we're caught up in the rapture and we're grabbing people with us! That is when the fight ends. This life is passing by and we need to get eternally minded. Our time is short so let's fight the good fight!

How did Nehemiah begin this tremendous task of rebuilding the walls? We see that his position was that of cupbearer to the king. He made sure that all the food that was prepared for the king was tested before it reached the king to insure the food wasn't poisoned. So we see that Nehemiah had a large responsibility and that the king trusted Nehemiah with his very life. Nehemiah knew what it meant to respect authority and because he walked in humility, we will see how he was blessed.

Nehemiah did not go up to the king and tell him he needed to leave his position to go work on the walls. We see that Nehemiah prayed in December and by April there was still no change in the situation.[3] Then, the king came to Nehemiah and asked why he had such a sad countenance? Nehemiah told the king that the walls of the Temple were falling down. The king asked Nehemiah what he would like to request. Nehemiah 2:9 shows us that not only was his request granted but he was allowed to take the captains of the army to protect him. In addition, the king gave him trees from the forest to rebuild the gates of the Temple. The king also gave Nehemiah letters of endorsement to be given to the governors of the territories. God did exceedingly abundantly above what Nehemiah could think or imagine!

Nehemiah had committed the work he had to do to the Lord so Nehemiah found favor with God and with man. He now had everything he needed to rebuild the walls of Jerusalem. The Lord has also provided us with everything we need to rebuild our own lives, by giving us His Son, Jesus Christ. All we have need of is found in Him.[4]

The joy Jesus had beyond the Cross was seeing us on the other side. Jesus saw eternally as He saw us reconciled to the Father. Whatever the struggles we are experiencing, we must *commit* them to God and then pray and *believe* Him to act on our behalf. We must not be moved by what we see and must be assured that God hears the cry of our hearts. Rest in the hope He has set before us and submit to His Lordship. In this way, your relationship with Him will be built.

Realize that when you do commit your way to the Lord, there will be opposition and you must be prepared to deal effectively with it. The opposition we face is the same opposition that Nehemiah and the children of Israel faced as they began to rebuild the walls. In Nehemiah 2:10, we see that the officials of the land were disturbed because Nehemiah had come to seek the well-being of God's people. Satan was disturbed in the same way when Jesus came to seek our well-being. Therefore the enemy will also attack you as you seek the well-being of God's people today.

Satan will attack you to the degree that you have an effective potential to be a warrior for God. If you have a desire to draw nearer to God and to help lead others to an intimate relationship with Jesus Christ, satan will resist you. But you must know that you can resist the opposition of the enemy. Greater is He who is in you. We can overcome the temptations and trials because Jesus Christ, the hope that is within us, has already overcome![5] We must trust God at His Word. We have the tools to withstand him for the weapons of our warfare are not carnal but mighty in God for pulling down strongholds.[6] God has equipped us with all we need to stand against the devil's tactics.

Come let's lift up the Body of Christ that the world will quit looking at us as a reproach.[7] How many of us will say, "Lord, take my heart; cleanse and purify me that I might be a vessel of honor, fit for Your use." How many of us will say, "Lord, get my life in order that I might join with the Body of Christ to seek the well-being of this generation"?

In Nehemiah chapter 4, we see that while the

children of Israel were repairing one part of the
wall, the enemy was attacking another part. The
attack came to the areas that were still torn down.
The same is true in our own lives. As we seek to
"build up" one area of our relationship with God,
the enemy will seek to distract and discourage us
by attacking another, *weaker* area of our lives. In
which areas is the devil seeking to pull you down?
Is it something related to your past? Is it a present
temptation? Be encouraged! God has given us
His Word and the power of His Spirit to overcome
in all situations.[8]

Nehemiah had a strategy to set guard against
the enemy's attacks. He placed people all along
the wall. Half of the people worked and the other
half guarded the work. The workers built with one
hand and held a sword with the other. We too,
should do the work of the ministry with one hand
and have the sword of the Spirit, the Word of God
in our other.[9]

We need to always "watch and pray" lest we
enter into temptation. We must be continually
on guard to stand against attacks against our
brothers and sisters in the Lord. God has given
us His Word, His Holy Spirit, and countless numbers of angels to ensure our success. We should
be determined to overcome the weaknesses in our
lives once God has revealed them to us. Remember, God's grace is sufficient.

Beginning in Nehemiah chapter 4, we see seven
oppositions that the devil tries to place in our path
once we commit to rebuilding our relationship
with God. The first opposition is ridicule and
mockery.[10] When you are ridiculed by others for
speaking God's Word, His truth, do not argue with
them. Don't be hindered but stand on God's

Word, knowing that this pleases Him.

The second opposition is the threat of the enemy's attack. The more the devil sees Jesus working in us, the more angry he becomes. He actively resists our work in building up the Body of Christ. Satan tries to bring fear and confusion upon God's people. If satan can succeed in distracting us, through thoughts of discouragement and fear that we won't be able to accomplish what we *know* **God** has called us to do, then he has hindered us. How did Nehemiah withstand this tactic? Nehemiah prayed. He submitted himself to God and because of his submission, God fought on his behalf.[11] God's people kept their eyes on Him knowing that since He called them to do the work, He would help them accomplish it. As the children of Israel concentrated on the work set before them, God protected them.[12] Their eyes were fixed on their God.

If our eyes get off of Jesus, then we can easily become discouraged. Discouragement is the third opposition the devil tries to put in our path. We see this happen to the children of Israel in Nehemiah 4:10. It will ultimately lead to complacency and then to compromise. When we are compromising in our walk with God, we will be ineffective in our work for God. How do we counter the attack of discouragement? We must always keep our eyes on Jesus and not allow our minds to dwell on the adversity of our situation. Remember our Great and Awesome God! You won't be afraid of the enemy when you realize who you are in God, and more importantly, who Christ is in you! Make sure the Word is powerful in your life.

The fourth opposition of the devil is the destruction of corporate unity through extortion. In

Nehemiah 5, we see Israel bringing its own people into bondage. Now God had delivered them out of bondage and did not want to bring them back into it. When we bring our brothers and sisters into bondage by usury, doctrine, any other means, we oppress the Body of Christ. In fact, we are dividing the Body of Christ.[13] Division destroys the unity of the faith and therefore we are ripping apart the very Body we say we want to rebuild. We must help build the corporate Body of Christ and be concerned with the well-being of *all* its members. If satan succeeds in dividing the Church, then we will be ineffective in fighting against his kingdom. As Jesus said in Matt. 12:25-26, a house divided against itself cannot stand. We must put away our carnality and become a Church family knitted together and working in unity. As we do, we will be effective in destroying our enemy and his camp!

The fifth opposition which will try to come against us is compromise. In Nehemiah 6:1-3, Nehemiah's enemies are trying to negotiate with him. They were seeking a settlement which would make both parties "happy". In other words, the children of Israel would make an alliance with their enemies. Through this agreement, they would seek their God but not build up the walls that would keep the enemy out. This would give the enemy-free entry. In other words, we may seek God but not build up a wall to keep the things of the world out of our hearts. When we are truly satisfied with God and what He is doing in our lives, we have no desire for the things the world has to offer. We will at that point, tell the devil, "We're serving God and moving on with Him"!

The sixth opposition that the devil will try to use is slander, as seen in Nehemiah 6:5-7. Through

false accusations, satan will try to bring a bad
report against us. If he deceives us into sin, we
become a reproach to the Name of the Lord. Many
prominent men of God have been attacked and
seduced this way in recent years. Their ministry
of Jesus to a lost world and even their own relationship with God has either been made totally
void or was greatly hindered. If however, a man
or woman of God is truly repentant, healing and
restoration to God and to the Church will occur.
Be careful not to become critical of your brothers
and sisters, for we are all vulnerable to attack. It
is what we do once we stumble that shows our
commitment to the Lord.

The seventh and final opposition we are going
to look at through our study of Nehemiah is fear.
In Nehemiah 6:13-14, Nehemiah says that the
enemy tried to make Him afraid to the point that
he would sin against God. Fear's aim is to lead us
into unbelief. Fear is the opposite of Faith. Don't
allow the devil to trick you into doubting God and
then give up. Why should you quit when the
Greater One lives in you? Are you truly trusting
in God to do a work in you and then through you?
It is because Nehemiah trusted in God that he did
not fall for the enemy's lies and sin against God.
It is faith that kept him going in spite of the
oppositions of the enemy.

Without faith it is impossible to please God and
we must stand on His promise which says we will
build the walls of the Temple. Order and stability
will come as we commit to getting the walls rebuilt.
We must first build up the walls in our own
relationship with God, for we are the Temples of
the Holy Spirit. Secondly, we must be willing to
be a part of setting things in order in the corporate

Body of Christ. Then, we will effectively seek the well-being of this lost generation.

NOTES:

1 Nehemiah 1:3-4
2 Approximately 4 months traveling time
3 Nehemiah 2:2
4 Colossians 2:10
5 John 16:33
6 2 Corinthians 10:4
7 Nehemiah 2:17
8 Luke 4:1-14
9 Hebrews 4:12
10 Nehemiah 4:1
11 1 Sam. 14:47; Deu. 1:30; 2 Chron. 16:9
12 Nehemiah 4:13-23
13 1 Corinthians 1:13-31; 3:1-4

11.

CHURCH QUAKE
The Lord's Provision During the
Shaking

"And it shall come to pass at that time that I will search Jerusalem with lamps, And punish the men who are settled in complacency, Who say in their heart, 'The Lord will not do good, nor will He do evil.'"

Zephaniah 1:12

Throughout scripture, Jerusalem is symbolic and a type of the Church today. I believe that God is speaking to us through Zephaniah in a prophetic manner. He is searching throughout the Church with the lamps of His Holy Spirit and shaking up those who are settled in complacency. By the light of the Holy Spirit, God is searching out the dross and rubbish in our lives to purge it from us. We need to allow Him to chisel away the stony areas of our hearts and challenge us to live beyond the status quo.

I have had a few opportunities to travel with a ministry team to Belize, Central America. Some of our team have been involved in street evangelism, some served on the Youth With A Mission base while others of us did humanitarian work. One year, my work consisted of building a pig pen and a ten-foot deep outhouse hole for a refugee woman and her family. While I dug the outhouse hole, I ran into a problem because after hours of digging, I kept hitting large boulders and rocks. After getting nowhere and with my hands bleeding from blisters, I asked the Lord to give me wisdom and strategy for the task. I laid down the large shovel-like chisel I was using and picked up a simple little hammer. Using the back of the hammer, I simply scraped around the perimeter of the large boulder until I could wedge in the chisel. I was then able to pry the boulder loose. It took three of us to pull it out of the hole with a rope. I thought this was the end of my problems, but I found there were other boulders also getting in the way of my objective. Now that God had given me the strategy to remove one large boulder, I was able to use the same strategy to overcome another, and another.

I was praying as I worked and began to see the analogy between my task and the Lord's work in us. The Lord has given us the strength and wisdom to remove the stony areas of our hearts. There are many stony areas of our lives that need to be removed. The outhouse hole I was digging will be filled again, but this time with outhouse waste. I wondered with sadness at how often the Lord had removed debris from our hearts, only to see us replace it with outhouse waste.

As God's Holy Spirit continues to search through the Church, and challenge us out of our complacency, we must fill our hearts, and minds with the things of God, not the waste of this world. He wants to give us a strategy for us to prepare for

His coming. We must do so, with great expectancy and anticipation of His return. Time is crucial. Time must be used effectively to reach this generation, which is perishing without Him. We must do something lest we do nothing in challenging others to emulate the Lord Jesus Christ. We cannot be lulled asleep like so many who are tired of hearing that Jesus is coming soon. Many have settled into that complacency and lifestyle of apathy.

People often criticize the failures of others, especially leaders in ministry, to make excuses for their own lack of desire in active service for the Lord. As we all do our part and plug into the Body of Christ, we build protective walls around the Church that make it a strong refuge for those coming out of the wilderness and out of this world.

There was a young man named Tony on the streets awhile back. Like many runaways (and many of the kids on your milk cartons), Tony ended up on the streets where he was quickly indoctrinated into homosexual prostitution. He had been there perhaps two years and was only 15 years old.

"Are you a homosexual?" I asked him.

"No, not at all," Tony answered.

"Then why are you doing this?" I asked.

"Because I like to eat!" he answered.

He said the only way he could support himself, just to eat and have a roof over his head, was to prostitute himself. Besides, he reasoned with me, the men were so good to him, giving him gifts and taking him places. I asked if any of them had the AIDS virus. He said he thought so. Life or death decisions, immorality, crimes—sin—by a 15-year-old who really just wants a roof over his head and something to eat.

Remember: Many people are searching and are spiritually hungry for anything. When people are famished, they will eat anything placed before them. We as Christians need to make sure that we have the solid, Christian food to serve them.

God so desires that not one should perish, He is going to great extremes to get our attention. We who are of finite thinking see only in the temporal. But God sees what is eternal. In order to make us effective witnesses for Him, able soldiers who can go into battles and defeat the enemy, He is going to take us through skirmishes that get our attention. It is during these times we learn to look to Him and rely on Him.

Over the past decade there has been a shaking in the Church with leaders' scandals, political fights, women's rights groups and homosexuals swaying Church doctrines, and the fight for our constantly erroding foundation of morals, ethics, and religious rights. The shaking can be a blessing or a curse to us. Hebrews 12:25-29 tells us that there will be such a shaking, only that which cannot be shaken will be left standing.

But through the shaking, the Lord has blessed us. How! Because He has proven Himself able to meet all our needs and even more. The shaking has caused us to see His perspectives and be more eternity-minded.

Deuteronomy 8:2-3 says, "And you shall remember that the Lord your God led you all the way these forty years in the wilderness, to humble you and test you, to know what was in your heart, whether you would keep His commandments or not." So He humbled you, allowed you to hunger, and fed you with manna which you did not know nor did your fathers know, that He might make you know that man shall not live by bread alone; but man lives by every word that proceeds from the mouth of the Lord.

God tries us and humbles us in order to make us stop relying on our own successes, strengths, abilities, and wisdom. God supernaturally shows us that true fulfillment and satisfaction in life comes only through our relationship with Him. When everything else seems hopeless and impossible, the Lord always proves Himself faithful.

If we, as the Body of Christ, will continue to yield to the correction and reconstruction of the Lord, then God will truly work out all things for us according to His Word "All things work together for good to those who love God, to those who are the called according to His purpose" (Rom. 8:28).

What is His purpose and how do we really know if we love Him? One of the highest forms of worship to God is obedience. It's what we do and act like during the wilderness times that will determine the expediting or the postponing of the plan He has for us. He really does want to work all things out for our good.

In the midst of all the strife, division, wars within the Body of Christ, confusion, God is doing His greatest work in us. The Lord will bring His sheep into line, both sheep and shepherds, except those who reject His final call. We must realize that in the midst of all the attacks and confusion, God still has His message of the Cross and Hope through Jesus Christ. With all the unleashing of the demonic and falling away within the Church, the Lord is preparing us for His return.

Judgement will begin at the house of God. The shaking begins there, too. Shepherds—ministers and leaders—who have been "off track" will be shaken and brought back through the Lord's stern but merciful, loving hand. Then the "fig tree" Christians who are only cosmetic in appearance but without bearing true fruit will be shaken. Those who will not repent will be moved aside for those who are preaching the true Gospel of Jesus Christ.

As those who suffer through God's refining, the "latter rain" of the Holy Spirit will fall on those true servants of the Lord who have felt forsaken and "weary in well doing" (Gal. 6:9; 2 Thess. 3:13). Those who have tried to serve the Lord with sincerity and integrity, who have been fighting the good fight with a genuine love for the sheep. They will begin to receive the stewardship and blessings to perpetuate the Gospel—exceeding and abundantly.

It has been a blessing to see these things taking place. By praying for, and not deserting many of our leaders, we have seen many return to the message of the cross and to the purity of the Word. Ministers are under constant attack. As we pray fervently for the Body of Christ and have a fresh experience at the Cross of Jesus Christ, we will see the outpouring of the Holy Spirit in true power.

In the last days, the sensual, demonic spirits of Hell will try to influence the Body of Christ. Let us consciously resist the devil so he will flee (James 4:7). When Gideon was looking for an army to fight the Philistines, God told him to choose only those men who drank from the river by lifting water to their mouth with their hands. Those who laid down to lap the water were not taken. We need to be like Gideon's army, staying ever so watchful for the evil that is in the land.

Similarly, Nehemiah's group of builders who restored the walls of Jerusalem built with one hand while holding a weapon in the other. We must be prepared to go into battle at all times.

But know this, that in the last days perilous times will come: For men will be lovers of themselves, lovers of money, boasters, proud, blasphemers, disobedient to parents, unthankful, unholy, unloving, unforgiving, slanderers, without self-control, brutal, despisers of good, traitors, headstrong, haughty, lovers of pleasure rather than lovers of God, having a form of godliness but denying its power.

2 Timothy 3:1-5

Part III
CROSSING THE JORDAN

*"Then he spoke to the children of Israel, saying:
"When your children ask their fathers in time to
come, saying, 'What are these stones?'*

*"then you shall let your children know, saying,
'Israel crossed over this Jordan on dry land';*

*"for the Lord your God dried up the waters of
the Jordan before you until you had crossed over,
as the Lord your God did to the Red Sea, which He
dried up before us until we had crossed over,*

*"that all the peoples of the earth may know the
hand of the Lord, that it is mighty, that you may
fear the Lord your God forever."*

Joshua 4:21-24

*Coming to Him as to a living stone, rejected
indeed by men, but chosen by God and precious,*

*you also, as living stones, are being built up a
spiritual house, a holy priesthood, to offer up
spiritual sacrifices acceptable to God through
Jesus Christ.*

1 Peter 2:4-5

12.

THE WAY, THE TRUTH AND THE LIFE

Jesus said that He was the Way, the Truth and the Life and that no man could come to the Father but through Him. We must remember that He also said that He came not to destroy the law but to be a fulfillment of it. He is our **Way** out of *Egypt (world)*, He is our **Truth** at *Mount Sinai (in the Wilderness)*, and He is our **Life** *in the Promised Land*. We cannot take only a part of Him, but *all* that He represents to us. If we only want Him as a way out of our problems or for fire insurance, yet reject Him at the place of *truth and obedience* in our lives, then we will die in the Wilderness and never enter into true victory.

Through the actual physical events of the past, God desires to teach us present-day spiritual truths. From the Exodus to the entrance into Canaan, Israel is made an "example" so we might learn from their mistakes.[1] The events of the wilderness wanderings therefore, become types and symbols—*teaching tools* which God uses to accomplish His purpose in our lives.

Now all Biblical typology has one express purpose and that purpose is to teach us about **Jesus**.[2]

Such "representative" teaching teaches us about
His Person (*who* He is), His Work (*what* He has
done for us) and His Character (what He is "like").
The teaching behind the Crossing of the Jordan is
no different. It demonstrates how we can apply
His Person, His Work and His Character to each
and every one of our lives. Furthermore, this
teaching is representative of something which
needs to occur in our hearts. Through the teaching of the Jordan, the Lord has drawn a "line" deep
inside our heart of hearts. And the question is,
will we *cross* that line?

In order to understand what the Lord desires to
teach us through the Crossing of the Jordan, it is
necessary to *first* understand what God was teaching the nation of Israel throughout the forty years
prior to this grand event! Now I could write
volumes of material concerning the typology con-
tained within the first five books of the "law"
(Genesis - Deuteronomy). Jesus is literally pro-
claimed in every story, in every event and sometimes in *every single scripture*. This is one of the
reasons why God commanded us to study His
Word; and for me, searching the scriptures is like
searching for hidden treasure. I really get excited
about learning more about Jesus!

There were basic reasons why Israel died in the
wilderness—the rejection of Truth at Mount Sinai.
I Corinthians 10:2 states that all Israel was "baptized unto Moses in the *cloud* and in the *sea*." The
"cloud" represents covering—the visible covering
of our Lord. The Lord Himself, withstood the
power of Egypt by "covering" Israel under the cloud
of His own presence.[3] The Baptism of the Crossing
of the Red Sea is a type of water baptism. It was
an open and public showing of leaving the world

behind, going through the waters and coming out different. The closing of the Sea behind Israel meant that Israel was prevented from going *back* into Egypt - from going back into the very bondage from which they were delivered. The Red Sea then, became a *barrier* which served a two-fold purpose in the *securing* of Israel's deliverance from bondage. Again, keep in mind that these things which happened in the "flesh" are typical of what happens to us in the *Spirit*, in Jesus! The pillar of cloud which represented the visible presence of Jehovah at the time of the Exodus has now become the indwelling Holy Spirit, the "visible" presence of God *within* us.[4] His presence in our lives constitutes a literal *hedge* around us.[5]

The Baptism in the Sea includes two points of interest from a spiritual perspective as well. In Jesus, through His death on the cross, and subsequent resurrection, Jehovah has literally *destroyed* the power of satan over us. So the first thing which the Baptism in the Sea represented in the spiritual realm was the absolute destruction of the power of darkness over us through Jesus' death, burial and resurrection!

Secondly, the closing of the Red Sea *behind* the children of Israel represented the closing of the "spiritual" doors which lead back to spiritual Egypt, or the bondage of sin. God closed the Red Sea so that Israel *couldn't* go back to Egypt even though they longed to in their hearts.[6] Jesus has done the exact same thing. In Jesus, we have been *spiritually* separated from Egypt. *Through* Jesus, God has placed the spiritual barrier of the Holy Spirit in our hearts in order to keep us from going back into the bondage and death from which He delivered us. We, like the Israelites, often long to go back into "Egypt" during certain wilderness times in our lives. The Holy Spirit was sent to *convict* us of sin.[7] Thus, with His convicting presence in our hearts, *true children of God* could never be happy living back in "Egypt". A true child of God can only be at peace when he or she is in right relationship with God.

In order to bring Israel into the Promised Land, God had to do two things. First He had to *deliver* Israel out of bondage and out from underneath the dominance of a foreign power. It remained for God to prepare His people to enter into their "rest". Having *delivered* His people, we see the Lord working to *prepare* His children to *occupy* and to *possess* the Land which He has promised them. It was time for Israel to go into *discipleship training*. God desired to disciple them so that one day they might receive the promise which He had previously ordained for them. Remember, you can take someone out of the world, but until you get the world out of his heart, there will not be true and lasting change. The Lord uses the wilderness times to build character in us and to remove the Egypt embedded in our souls (mind, will and emotions). In this character building process, we find the Lord wanting to build forth into His people, faith in Him as their Lord, their God and their Provider. God sought to instill faith in His people so that when they came to Sinai to be *taught* of God, they would *receive* His Word. He knows that it is human nature to *reject* instruction unless we first trust in, have respect for and "fear" or honor those who would instruct us. Again, this is what God's objective was through Israel's journey to Sinai and what His objective is with us today. God sought to instill certain attributes into

His people so that they would believe His Word
enough to *apply* it when they came to moments of
trial, temptations and quality decisions.

The giving of the Law from Mt. Sinai occurred
on the Day of Pentecost.[8] [9] Therefore, we have a
period of time here which is analogous to the
period directly following the Resurrection of the
Lord Jesus Christ. Acts 1:3 states that for forty
days Jesus "showed Himself alive" to His disciples
. . ."by many infallible proofs". During the same
period of time following the Passover, Jehovah
"showed Himself alive by many infallible proofs" to
the children of Israel as well! These "forty days"
were eventually stretched to *forty years* through
unbelief! Forty years of Jehovah "showing Himself
alive" to the children of Israel that they might come
to *believe* in His Word and to truly trust in *Him* for
provision, protection, victory and for "rest" amidst
a hostile and sin-sick world. Jehovah "showed
himself alive" to the children of Israel by many
infallible proofs as their Healer (Exodus 15:22-26
and Exodus 17:1-7); as their Provider (Exodus 15:
27-16:21), as their Victory Banner (Exodus 17:8-
16), and as **Lord.** It is He whom we submit to in
all matters pertaining to our lives (Exodus 18:1-
27). He showed Himself as **the God** who could
meet their needs (and ours, too!) in all areas of
life—physically and spiritually! Israel failed to
learn their lesson of faith and thus were sentenced
to *forty years* of "wilderness training" that they
might learn to trust in the Lord God of their fathers
and so receive those "*exceeding* great and precious
promises![10]

In Jesus, we also see it is necessary to *learn* of
Him, and to learn to trust *in Him* that we might
have the faith to go in and possess the land,

thereby finding rest for our souls. God doesn't
just lead us into the wilderness and expect us to
find our own way. He seeks to *prepare* us. He
also seeks to *disciple* us *so that the journey through
the wilderness of unbelief is as short as possible.*
In the discipling, the Lord is with us *every step of
the way*, working *first* to build our faith in Him
that we might stand (in victory) on the Evil Day
and go on to possess the Land!

MT. SINAI

At Mt. Sinai, God gave *the Law*. At Mt. Sinai,
God also taught His people. The Lord made Israel
to "sit at His feet" at the foot of His Holy Mountain
so they would learn of *Him*—to learn of all things
pertaining to "life and godliness". This teaching
encompassed all facts of civil *and* spiritual life.[11]

As I mentioned before, the giving of the Law
occurred on the Day of Pentecost. Here,God
sought to "empower" His people through the
teaching of His Word.   At Mt. Sinai, Israel experienced the very real and awesome *presence* of
God. The same was true (and is true today) with
the church in the second chapter of Acts. The
Church experienced that same awesome presence
and power of God through the *Baptism of the Holy
Spirit!* Thus, at Pentecost, God became (and becomes today!) more than a mere "concept". He
becomes a real, experiential and *living* God! We
see that these two events parallel each other
though they occur in totally different periods of
the Church's history.

The name of Moses is synonymous with the
giving of the Law at Mt. Sinai. It is also
synonymous with the manifest presence and
power of God revealed to His people.[12] God used

Moses to deliver ordinances to Israel in the name of Jehovah. God gave these ordinances because He desired to consecrate His people. The ordinances required commitment and absolute fidelity on the part of His chosen People.[13] A consecration to the Law meant a consecration to the perfect Word and Will of God *accompanied* by the effectual manifestation of the presence and power of that Word in and through their lives!

All of this of course, is typical of that consecration which Jesus was determined to accomplish in His disciples.[14] God has delivered us from "spiritual Egypt" in order that He might deliver us into the hands of His only Son.[15] The Son of God earnestly desires to consecrate us to Himself through *our* commitment to His Word and the effectual working of His power in and through our lives.

In the Old Testament, God was on the outside, looking in. In the New (and better) Testament, God is on the inside (and hopefully) flowing *out*.[16] Therefore, because Jesus was anointed with power from on High, so does He anoint us when we truly consecrate our hearts to be witnesses of Him and His Word!

Now again, please notice that all of this took place on the Day of Pentecost. Yet, the children of Israel still had not come to their Promised Land, their place of rest. After all of this good teaching, there is still more to come. Yes, there *is* life beyond Pentecost to the dedicated disciple of the Lord Jesus Christ. Pentecost is not the end of the Law to all those who believe. Tongues and the gifts of the Holy Spirit do not constitute the final dimension of the Christian experience.

Yet many Christians literally stop in their Chris-

tian walk. They stop, never to press on and dis-
cover the teaching of the Jordan. Therefore, like
Israel, they become "trapped" in the wilderness
and miserable in their Christian walk. God's plan
is to bring us to the Promised Land, not to leave
us at Mt. Sinai.

Those who do stop at Mt. Sinai can be seen
dying in the wilderness. They die spiritually of
carnal doctrines which are so typical of a Church
which is *out* of relationship with a Personal God.
This type of Church places its faith in a formula-
Christianity, rather than in a personal and living
God. This will never bring peace because peace is
the Person, Jesus Christ.

Jesus, our Prince of Peace, *never* fails. For-
mula-Christianity, however, never knows whether
their "white witchcraft" will ever work.

Christianity, therefore, is not a quick fix. It is
a living experience much like marriage. We have
to work at it on a daily basis. We can possess all
of the Gifts of the Spirit yet still be miserable
because we have yet to achieve that rest of faith.
There remains much more to Christianity then,
than Passover, the Red Sea and Mt. Sinai. There
still remains The Jordan which God wants us all
to cross in this life.

God has delivered us and now He desires to
prepare us to Cross the Jordan and receive our
Promised Rest. He didn't deliver us to let us die
in the wilderness. Remember, it's what we do
during the wilderness times in our lives that determines the expediting or postponing of our blessings.

The wilderness which the nation of Israel had
to pass through is signified by the trials which
Israel faced during the journey; they had to go

through this to come to a point of decision with God.[17] These trials represent the spiritual wilderness which each and every Christian faces in his or her journey to that spiritual Land of Promise. God had to reveal the heart of His people through these trials. As the heart is revealed, God shows us the barriers which we must overcome to receive our Promised Inheritance.

God revealed the *divided* heart of His people. This type of heart is not content solely with the things of God. It is a heart which does not derive its rest, peace and joy from a *personal relationship with God.*

The divided heart desires the things of this world *along with* the things of God. It requires the ways, the pleasures and the affections of this world in order to become *completely* fulfilled in the soul. In short, Israel still clung, in heart, to the idolatry from which they were physically delivered (Egypt).

It was therefore, God's desire to work this out of His people *before* He brought them to their place of decision. In this way, they would be *content* with the Good Land which He had prepared for them. The Lord knew that a divided heart would destroy His people spiritually and physically. As a *loving* Father, God worked to expose this sin so that His people would not fall prey to certain destruction!

Another kind of heart which God revealed in His people is a heart which is *rebellious* against His authority.[18] The authority could be in the form of Prophets, parents, husbands, governments, or the Holy Spirit Himself.[19] Victory and peace can only come through Jesus Christ and submission to *the* authority which is Lord of our lives.[20] Thus, for

Israel to triumph over the giants which were in the land, they simply had to trust in the Lord implicitly through submission and obedience to His express commands.[21]   Obedience is one of the highest forms of worship to God. A transformation has to first occur in our *hearts as* we act in obedience to God. Thus, our praise of Jesus, our victory in Jesus today is contingent upon this exact same principle. Praising His Name through mere show cannot successfully spearhead us through the wilderness and into the Promised land!

We must march through the wilderness proclaiming the fact that the Lord of Lords and the King of Kings became a *man* in order to die for our sins. In dying, He reconciled us to the Father that we also might become sons of the Living God through Him.   We are Sons and therefore, we will walk through this world's wilderness of idolatry and rebellion earnestly desiring with all of our heart to walk worthy of the vocation wherewith we are called.[22]

Jesus lived, suffered and died in a fiery furnace of affliction that *we* might be fruitful by taking up our cross and following Him; this is the mark of true discipleship.   Jesus desires to live and die through us that He might bring eternal life to those around us.

Because Jesus lives in us, so are we to overcome the idolatry and rebellion in our hearts and in the world around us. We must allow His perfect submission to the Father to live through us. In an idolatrous and rebellious world, we mirror His submission by overcoming evil with good and by never wearying in such well-doing. God wants us to keep our eyes fixed on our Sonship, our inheritance in Him rather than on the suffering and trials and tribulations which come into our lives. With our eyes so fixed upon Him, we can't help but be abundantly fruitful in this land.

How then do we enter into the Promised Land? How do we break through those barriers of idolatry and rebellion which ever seek to deny us of our rest? Minister unto *Him* as Sons and Priests in your personal relationship with Him. And as you journey through the wilderness of this world, lift up *Jesus* as your victory banner through the praise of Him who has won the victory over the power of sin (over us).

Count yourself dead to sin in Jesus. Be healed in the Name of Jesus and march securely as a new creature in Him, old things are passed away; behold, all things become new!

Lift up *Jesus* as the destroyer of the past which still leaves you with scars and which still keeps you in bondage. Lift up JESUS and walk safely and securely into your Promised Land of rest.

God's perfect plan, purpose and vision for His people is to bring us *out* of Egypt that He might bring us into the Promised Land. Therefore, God loves us so much that He does *not* leave us stranded and struggling in the wilderness. Rather, He *works* in our lives to purge the unbelief, the division and the rebellion out of our hearts that we might realize His perfect will for our lives.

He wants to lead us into the Promised Land! And what is this Promised Land? Well, to Israel it was an actual physical place of material prosperity, a land flowing with milk and honey. Thus, the Promised Land in essence, represents the *place* which God desires to brings us to. The Promised Land represents a prosperous place where we might dwell with Him while completing our pilgrimage on this earth.

Now the actual place of Canaan is only a Biblical type, a representation of what God desires to teach us about true prosperity, even that spiritual prosperity which is in His only Beloved Son. Thus, in spirit, Canaan represents the place where God desires to bring us in *our relationship with Him!*

The Lord used Israel's journey to teach us about our inheritance in Him. *The* inheritance which is the *end* of our faith. *The* inheritance which represents the ultimate goal of the commandment. And this inheritance is a Person, the Lord Jesus Christ.

Jesus is our inheritance and this is the joy for which He suffered on the Cross to bring us to Himself, that through Him we might become sons, even co-heirs *with* Him. We are co-heirs of a personal and intimate marriage relationship of such beauty and of such holiness which brings total contentment in every area of our lives. Through submission, loving trust, unqualified committal and obedience to Him in all areas of our life, we can truly possess direction, peace and joy in *this* life. We can truly possess rest no matter *what* kind of persecution we may be experiencing. True rest comes in our relationship with Him as we carry out the work of the ministry to a sick and dying world.

Jordan is the place where self needs to die daily, where we need to take up our cross on a daily basis and follow Jesus. We need to follow Jesus and die to our own doubts and fears, our own ambitions and desires. We have got to crucify any fear which seeks to prevent us from dying to self and living wholeheartedly for Jesus!

We need to understand that we are *not* right with God if we still long in our hearts to sin. We need to understand that we are still in the wilderness if our affections are in this world and we are living like they are. We need to understand that we can never Cross the Jordan while we are still longing in our hearts to go back to Egypt oscillating between our desire for Him and our love for this world.

Crossing Jordan therefore, means reaching a place in our relationship with the Lord whereby we don't want to go back to Egypt. We do desire to joyfully embrace His will for our lives rather than our own. Crossing Jordan is where Jesus truly sits on the throne of our hearts. It's a crossing of a line in our hearts whereby we walk toward loving the Lord with all of our hearts with all of our souls and with all of our might. We should not look back at our former love for the things of this world.

In order for us to go into and possess the land, as Jesus called us to do, we must first be willing to Cross the Jordan—whatever the cost! Let's put away our divided hearts once and for all and be that mighty, world-shaking extension of His hand that He has called us all to be.

NOTES:

[1] 1 Corinthians 10:6-11
[2] John 5:39; Luke 24:44; Hebrews 3 and 4
[3] Exodus 14:19-20
[4] John 14:15-21; Revelation 3:20
[5] Job 1:8-10
[6] Exodus 16:2; Numbers 11:4-6
[7] John 16:7-15
[8] Exodus 20
[9] Acts 2
[10] 2 Peter 1:1-4

[11] Recorded in Ex. 19:2-40; 38; the Book of
Leviticus & Num. 1:10- 11
[12] Exodus 34:27-35; 2 Cor. 3:1-18
[13] Exodus 32 & 34 #3
[14] Luke 12:50; Matt.3:11
[15] John 5:17-47; Matt.28:18-20
[16] Galatians 2:20; Phil. 1:21
[17] Numbers 11 &12
[18] Num. 12; 14:5-12; 16
[19] Romans 13:1-7
[20] Phil. 2:1-11; Heb. 5:7-9; James 4:1-10
[21] Num. 13:30; 14:6-9
[22] Eph. 4:1

13.

THE HIGH COST OF LOVE

God did not bring Israel out of Egypt in order to abandon His people in the Wilderness. The Lord does not deliver us from the bondage of sin in order to forsake us as we seek to draw closer to Him. There is a *High Cost* to the Love which He exhibits in the scriptures. There is a *High Cost* to the Love which He shows to us each and every day of our lives! We need to realize what it took for Him to secure our souls that He might embrace us forever as His children. We need to *understand* how high a cost that was for Him to voluntarily offer Himself up on our behalf!

What should we do therefore, with so precious a gift, so great a salvation? Should we crucify Jesus over and over again by continuing in sin; or, should we allow Him to purge, refine and polish us so that we will *enjoy* His presence as we walk in victory? God *wants* us to enjoy His presence, you know; therefore, I believe that the answer to this question is quite obvious.

To some however, the answer to this question is not so obvious. There are those within the Church who want God, but earnestly desire what the world has to offer, as well. These are treading

upon dangerous ground. These are engaging in a
tight rope act upon the fine line of God's grace.
The Word of God emphatically states that those
who *knowingly* practice sin as a regular part of
their lifestlye are *not* Born-again.[1] I repeat, these
have *not* truly humbled themselves before the Lord
thus, receiving the presence of His indwelling
Spirit.

Now it is not anyone's job to judge another
person's "salvation". Whether we are lost and
dead in our sins, or whether we are a Christian
living in rebellion to God (as was King Saul), the
answer is still *Jesus*! The answer is still repentance of sin and faith in the Lord Jesus Christ.
Therefore, let us leave this type of judgement to
Him, who *only* is able to discern the hearts of men.
Let us leave this type of judgement to God and
simply be faithful to minister Jesus to those who
are bound by the cords of their own sins whether
they be lost or saved.

Yet, we need to love people enough to confront
them with their sins, *as God leads*. Those who sin
and choose not to repent are treading a fine line
concerning God's grace. Those who willingly
remain insensitive to the conviction of the Holy
Spirit are flirting with danger, as well as the state
of their eternal soul.[2] One who continues to practice sin will be pulled further and further apart
from God. These individuals desperately need to
heed the admonition which the Apostle Paul gives
to the Corinthian church in 2 Corinthians 13:5.
Here he admonishes the Church to "examine yourselves, whether you be in the faith; prove your own
selves . . ." The Apostle Paul penned this challenge
to the Corinthian church because He knew that
these were lost people as well as saved people

attending this New Testament Church. Do you hear what I'm saying?

So the Apostle Paul *challenges* the Corinthians. He says, "*prove* yourselves. Are you really "in" the faith? Are you truly Born-Again? Examine yourselves!" The Lord had Paul issue this challenge because there were people in this church who desperately needed to take a look at their lives and sincerely   search   their   hearts   concerning   the things of God. The fact is that there are *still people today* in the church who need to search their hearts and minds concerning the things of God in their lives. The fact is that there are too many "tight rope" acts going on within the church and such hypocrisy is seriously affecting our witness to this lost and dying world!

Well, if God doesn't want this lukewarm, "tight rope" style of Christianity, then what *does* He want? I have said it before and I will say it again, God wants *relationship*, right relationship with *you*! God wants *commitment* to *His* will and purpose for our lives. God wants *obedience* that He might bless us beyond all blessings which this world has to offer!

What does God want? God wants a *perfect heart* within us. Yes, we may stumble and fall, but we can choose whether or not we want to remain *in* that sin. The perfect heart of God will eagerly choose to *forsake* that sin and trust in the power of God's Holy Spirit to enable him to walk in perfect obedience to God in that specific area of his or her life! The perfect heart of God within us becomes *grieved* at sin as God Himself grieves over sin. This is the heart of true repentance. This heart becomes so grieved over sin that it eagerly seeks forgiveness that it might *rejoice* before the Father in love and in obedience! And again, the heart that remains *in*sensitive to the convictions of the Holy Spirit, is the *divided* heart which is separated from God and in desperate need of *examination.*

So what is the difference, or what *makes* the difference between the perfect heart (of God) and the divided heart (of our own self)? Why does one Christian exhibit a "perfect heart" while another exhibits a "divided heart"? I submit to you that the sole reason for the difference between the two hearts is their *love* for God. One heart is relatively cold and indifferent towards the Lord.[3] The other heart, however, perceives the incredibly *High Cost of the Love* which reached out and sovereignly plucked us out of the jaws of eternal death! Of such quality was the Love of the "woman" in Luke 7:41-50, and of such quality was the Love of the woman who anointed Jesus for His burial in Matthew 26:6-13. This perfect heart of Love toward the things of God is why Jesus stated that this act would be preached for a "memorial" wheresoever the Gospel was to be preached. Yes, Jesus *did* honor this woman by saying this, but His primary intention was to draw attention to the type of heart which pleases God the most; it is the type of heart that will produce a *true* disciple *wherever* the Gospel is preached!

To illustrate the high cost of the Father's Love towards us, I would like to share a story with you. This story is about a father's sacrificial love for the lives of others. Now this father's sole job was to operate a draw bridge which allowed the train to pass by his station each day. His son loved him very much and he went to work with his father as often as possible.

One day the father lost track of his son and he

began to worry. He searched and searched but couldn't find him. The time to pull the lever which lowered the bridge was drawing near. The lives of the passengers on that train depended upon the man doing his job. Suddenly, the father noticed his son down in the shaft, caught in the gears.

The father then had a choice to make. The train would soon be crossing and the father did not have time to stray and free his son. The time to pull the lever had almost come. He could save his son by not pulling the lever. The people on the train weren't aware of what was happening. They didn't even know that each day the lives of many rested upon this man's faithfulness to do his job, to pull that lever.

This father looked down again at his son and his heart began to ache. If he chose to rescue his son, the people on the train would surely descend into the large gully and die. The painful realization of his responsibility suddenly became apparent. As he pulled that lever, he began to cry out loudly over the screams of his son who was being ripped apart by the gears below. At the cost of his own beloved son, he had saved the lives of many. The people on that train passed by totally unaware of the price which had been paid to guarantee their safety. The faithfulness of this one father had given them the gift of life.

The faithfulness of God our Father, has also guaranteed *us* the gift of life, the gift of *eternal* life! Through the loving but painful sacrifice of His only Son, God has set us free from the bondage of our sin so that we could enjoy a personal relationship with Him. Let us therefore *meditate* upon the price which Jesus paid to secure us so great a salvation. Let us meditate and be *thankful* for what He has done on our behalf. Let us *not* be like the people on that train who were totally unaware of the price that was paid to ensure their very lives.

There is another story which illustrates a similar point. This story is about a sinking boat. This boat had a large gaping hole in its hull and water was pouring in. The crew was bailing out the water as fast as they could but the situation was only getting worse. The captain needed a volunteer to help plug the hole. Whoever volunteered understood that he would possibly be risking his own life so that the rest of the people might live. The silence was long and painful; finally, someone did volunteer. It was the captain's own son! He said, "dad, I'll do it." As a father, it was a painful decision. As the captain however, he had no choice but to consent for the good of all concerned.

Now this son might have spoken words that were similar to those which Jesus spoke to His father. "Father, your people will perish if something isn't done" (just as the wages of *our* sin is eventually, eternal death!). "They are in danger of sinking (just as we are bound by the cords of our own sins), but I volunteer to go down and save them." And so, this son went down into the water and finding nothing to plug the hole, put his arm into it and became a human plug sacrificing his own life.

None of the great men of the Bible could accomplish what Jesus *Himself* accomplished for us on the Cross. Only *Jesus* won the right to restore you and me to a right relationship with God. God is saying to us today, "I died to give you hope. I died to give you vision for your life. Don't let My death for your sake be in vain. Don't allow yourself to perish in the wilderness. Realize that those "Goliaths" in your life are just there to refine you spiritually and to draw you closer to Me. *Trust Me* and Cross the Jordan. Enjoy My presence in the valleys as well as on the mountain tops. True peace and true rest in this life come only from abiding in *Me*.[4] Remember, I will *never* leave or forsake you. Only look to *Me* and you will pass through the wilderness under the cloud of My own presence!

Matthew 13:44-46 shows us how precious and how desirable we are in the eyes of our own heavenly Father! Jesus Christ took great joy in "selling all that He had" in order to purchase a land that had a great hidden treasure.[5] He sold everything He had in order to purchase that one pearl of great price. Now we all know that He *Himself* is that great hidden treasure and that one pearl of great price in the eyes of the Father. However, the Word of God teaches that *we* are *His* special treasure and pearl of great price. Therefore, was He willing to give all that He had that He might purchase us.

Jesus saw us as the polished pearl that we would one day become in Him. We were the hidden treasure which no one but Jesus saw hope in.[6] Jesus alone, saw our potential in Him! Therefore, He purchased us with His own blood.[7] We no longer belong to ourselves then, we belong to *Him*. We are the Temple of *His* Holy Spirit. Therefore, we should allow Him to work the sins out of our lives that separate us from the fellowship that He so earnestly desires to enjoy with us in this life.

Jesus is not a master who puts us in bondage even though He does "own" us through the price that He paid with His own blood. He is a master

who gives us *freedom,* freedom to reign *with* Him!
He *bought* us that He might *free* us! Therefore,
don't be purposeless in your living. When you see
who Christ is *in you,* you will find out your purpose
in this life. And whether you ascend to the "mountain top" or descend into the "valley", you will know
that you belong to Him and that *nothing* will ever
separate you from His love and care.[8]

There are so many distractions which we face
in this life. The principalities and powers of this
world *continually* try to make the love of our hearts
wax cold. We need to come back to the place of
realizing just *who* our "First Love" is on a daily
basis! We can do this by remembering the cost of
Calvary. We can do this by remembering Jesus'
look of love as He stumbled up the hill to Calvary
having been rejected and beaten to a pulp. How
high a cost it was for us to be able to receive His
Love!

If we would but remember *Jesus* (and the Cross
which He bore) every time that we go through a
struggle, then our "light afflictions" would not
seem so difficult. The greatest change in our lives
comes as God *disciples* us in the midst of our
trials! *Give* Him free reign then, and remember the
high cost of the Love that set you on the road of
eternal life with Him!

Dave Roever was a man who was badly injured
during the war in Vietnam. His face was severly
scarred. He tells a story of when a friend of his
broke his guitar. This story shows a comparison
of the trials which *we* go through, to the pain
which *Jesus* suffered while on the Cross. Dave's
friend felt so bad about it that for days he kept
apologizing for his carelessness. Finally, Dave
couldn't stand it anymore. He grabbed his friend's

hand and placed it upon his own face. He said, "When you have gone through *this* kind of pain, and can understand all that this face has gone through, then you would see that this broken guitar will never compare." If we would realize the high cost of the Love which purchased our souls, then our "broken guitars", our frustrations, and our hurts would never seem quite so bad. Instead of driving us away from Jesus, they would draw us *closer* to Him.

As we draw closer to Jesus in this way, during the times of our trials, we will then be in a position to see God turn our struggles and hurts into something good for us and glorious for Him.[9] In the midst of our trial we will be able to say, "Lord, I know all things work together for good for those that love you and are called according to your purpose." Therefore, we can either indulge in self-pity and bow down to discouragement and defeat; or we can say, "Lord, I know the cost you paid to show me how much You love me", and rise to victory!

A true disciple asks God how he or she can *learn* from the trial which is being experienced. A true disciple knows that *Jesus* is the Rock on whom we lean and in whom we trust. A true disciple realizes the high cost of the Love which went to the Cross and died for our sins in order to ensure an eternal life for us. A true disciple *understands* that Jesus was literally poured out like water for our sakes.

As Jesus hung on that cross, He began to dehydrate. His muscles began to atrophy. As His muscles atrophied, they lost their ability to support His bones and ligaments. His bones came out of their sockets. His heart burst, while His lungs filled and then collapsed. He died a painful death and paid for the times that you and I would break His heart. He paid for the times that you and I would rebel against Him, rejecting Him and denying Him the right to be Lord *over every area* of our lives. It was a *humiliating* death for the God of this universe to subject to Himself.

Oh, if we would only come to the place of our "First Love" in Him. Then, when our hearts are overwhelmed within us, He would set us upon the Rock that is higher than ourselves (Psalm 61:1). With a right heart and a proper understanding of the high cost of Calvary we can truly say, "Lord, lead me to the Rock, to the Rock that is higher; lead me to the Rock that is higher than I." With full assurance, we will *know* that He hears us and that He is leading us to that steady Rock during the midst of our storms. With a proper *daily* understanding of the high cost of the love which purchased our souls, we will stand firm *in* His love, ever seeking to conform to His image, rather than the image of this world! **Focus in on the "High Cost of His Love" for nothing, absolutely nothing will ever compare again!**

NOTES:

[1] 1 John 3:9; 1 Cor. 6:9-20; Prov. 6:16-19
[2] Romans 8:1; Heb. 10:26
[3] Matthew 24:12
[4] John 15
[5] Matthew 13:44; Hebrews 12:2
[6] Matthew 13:44
[7] Acts 20:28
[8] Romans 8:28-39
[9] Phil. 3:8-14

14.

SPARKING REVIVAL

How often have we looked back at some of the Great Revivals in history! Revivals, which men like Spurgeon, Wesley, Finney and Tozier have helped to bring about. We look back and we tend to think, "Oh, if we could have revival like that today!"

We can certainly pray, "Lord, bring revival to our lives, our city and our nation!". We must realize, however, that with revival comes *responsibility*. Along with responsibility comes the need for *action*. Yes, in order to bring revival we must first act on our faith.

Revival in China, Vietnam and other countries around the world comes in the midst of persecution. However, God does not desire persecution to be the primary spark for revival in our hearts. God desires that revival come as a result of our own willingness to become consecrated and committed vessels unto Him. We need to be willing vessels that allow His rivers of living water to flow through us to a lost and dying world.

Unfortunately, instead of coveting this willingness, we tend to lapse into complacency. We tend to become comfortable in the world in which we live. This indulgence in worldly comforts *prevents* revival from coming. When our hearts become lifted up in our own wealth, possessions, our own security and we tend to *forget* the Lord.[1] When we forget the Lord, our love for Him grows cold. Our desire and hunger to keep His commandments begins to fall away. We thus, inadvertently call for *judgment* to come upon the House of the Lord.

So do we realize what we are really saying when we pray, "Lord, bring *revival* to our land!"? When we pray such a prayer, we must come to grips with the responsibility to allow God to *shake* us out of our coldness for His love and out of our complacency in keeping His commandments. We must *act* through *repentance* of our worldly ways. When a church has become cold and complacent, persecution is the only means by which God can purge the apathy which has so infected His people.

God does this out of His love.[2] He refines us because He desires the best for us.[3] Consequently, that means that our finances might begin to be shaken up. We might even become dissatisfied in our jobs, school, with our friends, and the "status quo" of our lives. Why? It is because a holy hunger may begin to spring up through the sovereign call of God! Praise God! This holy hunger becomes a living testament of Christ; thus, a living sacrifice unto God that will never be satisfied with the things of this world! If we are truly born-again into the Kingdom of God, we will never be satisfied with anything other than an intimate and uncompromising walk with the Lord Jesus Christ.

We can possess all of the money in the world, have the happiest of marriages, the best of friends and even attend the best of churches. However, if we are not sold-out in our relationship with Jesus, we will never be truly satisfied in our hearts! If we are not answering God's call to revival in our hearts, we are destined only to *misery*. This misery may lead to an eventual backsliding. If you are crying out, "God, I need to hear from you." He is saying, "I have already given you a command, seek Me with all of your heart and you *will* find Me."[4] "Obey Me and I *will* manifest Myself to you."[5] I can assure you that we will have no true and lasting peace until we answer the call that God is making on our hearts today.

Now don't confuse the call to revival with the call to go into full-time ministry. This is not what the Lord is saying in these Last Days. God is simply desiring His children to become willing vessels that He can live through. Are you called to a job, marriage and family? Are you called to "ministry"? Wherever we are called, God simply desires us to fill our lives up with *Him* that we might manifest His love to whomever He has placed in our path.

Ultimately however, every born-again believer in Christ Jesus should pray about a ministry of "helps" with existing full-time ministries. Getting involved in this way not only helps to further the Gospel, but it also helps us to keep our "Godly perspective" in the midst of a self-indulgent society. In other words, getting involved helps us to remember why we are here as Christians.

We don't get involved with a particular ministry just because we want to boast about what we are doing for God. That kind of spiritual pride is just as bad as complacency because we are doing it for all of the wrong motives. Rather, we should be getting involved in the work of the Gospel for the

sole motivation of honoring and pleasing God!
When we get involved with this kind of heart
attitude, then we become the ones who are ministered to.[6] No longer are we representatives of a
selfish, self-centered Gospel. We become representatives of a Gospel that is based upon reaching
out to others with the heart of God Himself and
this is the meaning of being a vessel that is fit for
His use.

If we become involved in a ministry or if we go
on a short-term missions with the attitude, "*I'm*
going to be a blessing to them. *I'm* going to go
there and preach to them", then we are basing
our works on self-righteousness and not on the
love of God. This is an abomination to God because
such an attitude is based solely on pride in one's
own abilities. In actuality, we should be saying,
"Lord, thank You for the honor and the privilege
of allowing me to be a part of the ministry. Lord,
thank you for the least little bit which You allow
me to do in Your Name!"

When this becomes the attitude of our hearts,
every time we minister to others then we receive
ministry back in like kind. When this becomes the
attitude of our hearts, then every envelope we lick
and every label we stick on for the Kingdom of
Heaven's sake becomes well-pleasing in the eyes
of God. When we know that we have pleased God,
then we do experience true peace in our hearts.

The same is true with tithes and offerings. We
don't give because we want to bless the local
congregation or the ministry that we are involved
with. We give to bless *God*. We give in obedience
to *His* command. We give because it's a *privilege*
and an *honor* to participate with Him in this way
to further the Gospel!

With this kind of heart attitude in ministry, we will see the whole concept behind what it means to be a Christian, change. We will see the self-centered Gospel of self, change to the *true* Gospel of the Lord Jesus Christ! We will become living testaments, through which, God's Holy Spirit really can move! Revival will take place in our own hearts as we seek to bring revival to others. The first step in sparking revival is not to look back to the great revivals of the past, but rather, it is to look to the present. It is to look at our hearts right now and ask "What are we going to do today and in the days to come?"

Is there a remnant today that really desires to honor God and seek Him with all of their heart? Do we really believe that God can turn our own hard hearts around? Do we believe that He can still move upon a city, a state, or a nation with His own convicting presence? What makes us doubt Him so? Our doubt comes from within ourselves. We *say* that we want revival, yet we are not willing to pay the price. We are not yet willing to take up our cross in all sincerity and truth and follow Jesus!

The Lord is saying today that if we truly desire revival, we must first be willing to take up our cross and follow Him. We must first be willing to become *living* sacrifices unto Him. Our flesh screams out against such consecration and commitment.

We don't want to become living sacrifices who take up their cross to follow Jesus. Yet, once we obey God, the greatest fulfillment which we have ever known begins to take place in our hearts. Once we make that commitment, we will wonder why we ever fought it to begin with!

Jesus said that His "meat" was to do the will of Him that sent Him.[7] Jesus said that the harvest has been ripe since His own earthly ministry.[8] I believe that the Spirit of God is urging us to manifest this same heart attitude today. Teenage youth gangs are on the upswing. Witch covens are proliferating and are becoming more and more popular in schools as well as in society itself. Drug trafficking and drug addiction is still wreaking havoc in the lives of young and old alike. Homosexuality and sexual immorality continue to seduce our young and bring ruin to their lives while the Church continues to languish in its own complacency and compromise.

Yet, I believe that there is a remnant. I believe that God is raising up vessels of honor that will stand for His holiness and righteousness. He will birth a spirit upon all of those who will stand up and say, "God, I *want* to be committed. Lord, I *want* to be faithful no matter how I feel. Live through me, Jesus, and help me to surrender to you with *all my heart*." This is the vision that God desires us to take hold of today, for this is the vision which will spark revival in each and every one of our hearts!

Do you believe that revival can come to your city? If so, will you take on the responsibilities involved when the Lord starts bringing in the harvest? Will your faith take *action*? What will we do if all of the gangs in our cities come to Jesus? What will we do with them? What will we do with the homeless who come to Christ? What *churches* are we going to put them into? *What will happen* when we get away from the institutionalized, status-quo of religious organizations? Will we make ourselves available to God in order to minister to these people? Will we allow Him to make disciples of us so that we will be properly equipped to make disciples of them once they come to know Jesus?

Our goals must change! Our goals must not be to bring the harvest to our own names, institutions, and self-centered Gospel. Our goal needs to be to bring them to Jesus. Our goal needs to be to make them disciples of the Lord and not to make them disciples of a particular doctrine or of a particular denomination. We need to really see what the responsibilities are when we pray for revival; we must be prepared to back up our faith with action. We must be prepared to become that living sacrifice and to act on our faith before God will trust us with the outpouring of His Holy Spirit of revival!

In the last ten years, the Lord has raised up numerous ministers and ministries across the land who are not concerned with numbers and they are not concerned with bringing glory to a particular person or denomination. They are concerned about giving glory to *God*. They are concerned about making *disciples* and making a true stand for holiness and righteousness today. This is *the remnant* and God sees the desire of their hearts. God sees that their desire is His desire and thus, will He bless them with the anointing oil of His own presence!

I believe that the church is at a crossroads now, a pivotal point in our ministries and in our lives. Many are being destroyed through their own indulgence in the worldly pleasures of sin. Others are being seduced into complacency through their own compromise of God's Word. God warned us about this "coming apostasy" before it happened

and He is giving us a chance to come out of it now.[9]
We are at a crossroads; will we go on as religious
devotees who are caught up in our own petty
rivalries? Or will we go on as *true spiritual
revivalists* for Jesus seeking God on behalf of our
families, our cities and even our nation? God is
calling us as a generation of people that will not
live on the laurels of yesterday's revivals. God is
calling us to learn from the past while we seek Him
concerning a fresh direction for the future.

Yes, it is easy to get settled into a specific kind
of ministry and to get used to doing things in a
specific sort of way. It is easy to look back and say,
"Look how far we have come." However, God wants
to break through all of that and bring us to the
point where we are focusing on *Him* and following
Him. This is the only way His Church can be an
effective Church in this generation. We are only at
a beginning today. God showed me that what we
have been doing as a ministry during these past
ten years is only a taste and a preparation for the
anointing which He desires to pour out upon us
today, *if* we will obey Him!

In the book of Ezra, two and half to three million
Jews had the opportunity to come out of Babylon,
only fifty thousand actually answered God's call.
Babylon represents the world with all of its seductive ways and with all of its pleasures of sin. In
many ways, we live in a society that is like a
modern day "Babylon" and God is making the
same call to the church today, as He did to the
Jews of Ezra's time. The question is, how many
of us will answer God's call in this day and time?
How many of us will come out of "Babylon" and
return to build a temple that is truly pleasing to
the Lord our God? How many of us will forsake

sin and not be caught up in the seductive lures of this life, in order to make an uncompromising stand for Jesus today?

There is a "Jezebel Spirit" that is attacking the Church at this time. The Bible says in Revelation 2:18-29, that those who commit adultery with this spirit will be cast into a bed of *great tribulation* with her. Anyone of us who claims to be a Christian, yet chooses to partake of this Babylonian spirit will find himself in areas of sickness, defeat and unfulfillment. If we are in this state, we will be completely devoid of joy because we are not fulfilling what God has called us to do.

If we find that we have an unfulfilled hunger and thirst, we need to begin to *discipline* our flesh in order to seek the things of God. We need to get involved as true servants of the Lord in all humility and truth. We have been born-again to please God and to serve God by proclaiming the Good News. If we settle back in our complacency and in our compromise and cease to proclaim the Good News of Jesus Christ, then the unsaved will not find the eternal life which is in Him! In effect, *our* compromise and complacency will bring *their* blood onto our hands! We must not therefore, be satisfied with the comforts of this world. We must forsake the bondage of this world and concentrate on building the temples that God has given us.

When we become born-again into the Kingdom of God, God desires us to concentrate on building our *spiritual* houses, our spiritual temples in Him, rather than our position in this world. When we become born-again, God desires us to seek the *eternal* things of His truth, rather than the temporal things of this world. Yes, we need to learn from this particular period in Israel's history. If we are experiencing "heavy resistance" in building our temples in the Lord, in walking with Him day in and day out, then we should not give up and just live to satisfy our own fleshly desires. We need to press on and fight that good fight of faith. We must trust God to defeat that resistance for us so that we can continue about our business of building His temple within us!

How many of us have been serving God only to turn around and begin to serve ourselves because of some difficulty which came into our life? We replace the pursuit of God's desires for the pursuit of our own. Pretty soon, we begin to focus our lives on what pleases us, rather than what pleases God. This is the message of the book of Haggai. Sometimes it is easier to stop building our spiritual temples and pursue our own interests, rather than fight that good fight of faith and hold faithful to God's will for our lives. If we allow ourselves to become discouraged and consequently succumb to this spirit of complacency, then we will fall into the same state of spiritual lethargy that the remnant of Israel did in Haggai's day.

It is time to become preoccupied with the work of the Lord in our lives, rather than with our own building projects. It is time to become concerned with the beautification of the Lord's temple within us, rather than with our own "houses". When our priorities become misplaced, our "labor" in this life is no longer blessed by God.[10] Only when we put the Lord *first* in the work that He has called us to do, do we experience His hand of blessing upon us.[11] This is the place where God is bringing the Church today. We have got to choose to place His priorities first in our life. We have got to stop and re-evaluate what direction our lives are taking.

Much of the tribulation and persecution that we experience in this life is not so much the attack of the devil as it is God trying to get our attention. God wants His blessings to flow in our lives again if we would but only put His priorities first in all that we think, do and say!

In the first chapter of Haggai, God chastises His people for taking care of their own personal affairs and neglecting His priorities in their lives. In the second chapter of Haggai, the Lord encourages His people to be strong and to be diligent about the work which He desires to complete in their lives. Many churches equate the work of the Lord with being faithful in the tithe and in the offering. However, God is not after our money; the Lord is after our *hearts*. God doesn't want control just of our finances. He wants control of *everything*. God wants *every* part of our lives submitted to Him, so that He can be the Lord of our lives completely! This includes allowing Him to be the Lord of our careers, our finances, our marriages, the Lord of all! When we submit to His Lordship over our lives, we become servants of Jesus Christ no matter what vocation, ministry or state He has called us to!

Revival can come when we *know* that Jesus Christ is God of our lives. When God sees that we have a true servant's heart, He will equip us with the boldness, the confidence and the *power* to do what He has called us to do. Why then, are we afraid? We need fear no man, neither the principalities and powers of this world. We can believe God to take our cities for Jesus. If we have the desire to please God by bringing more children into His Kingdom, then He will bless our efforts abundantly. We are *God's* representatives in this

world and when we agree with Him concerning His
will for our lives, we can destroy the works of the
devil, no matter where they are manifested in our
lives.

We can send shock waves through our cities.
We can turn the world upside down for Jesus even
as the early church did.[12]   We may not feel it
physically, but I guarantee that we can send a
shock wave *spiritually* through this world that will
begin to manifest itself in the physical. All God
needs to do this, is hearts that are yielded to Him.
He needs hearts that are willing to follow Him
wherever and *how*ever He leads. Then, the Lord
Himself, will be that shock wave that literally turns
this world upside down as He moves and lives
through us.

We cannot expect God to do miracles in our
hearts as well as in our cities if we continue to
remain indifferent to the movement of His Holy
Spirit in our lives. If we **truly believed**, then we
wouldn't *remain* indifferent and apathetic. If we
truly believed, then we would realize the power
there is in the spoken Word of God. If we **truly
believed**, we would realize the seriousness of the
war which we are involved in.

We need to begin walking in righteousness and
holiness before Him. We need to see the weaknesses of the Body of Christ as *God* sees them and
begin to do what we can to build up the Body of
Christ. You know you could be the very one who
is willing to pay the price to bring revival to your
city or town. Therefore, even though you may feel
alone, you could make all the difference in the
world. Your prayers alone could be the effect on
that loved one or city.

God is looking for a remnant that will do

whatever He asks of them. He is looking for a Church that is a *Living Testament* of the Lord Jesus Christ. He is looking for the faithful, the available, the *willing disciple*, who will simply **believe God**. God will honor the heart that is willing to say, "I'll do whatever you want me to do, Lord!" This is the life that **God** will use!

It is the time of the latter rain and God said that the latter rain would be greater than the former rain. If you think the revivals of the past were awesome, just wait until you see what God has for the future. The future begins *now* and we can be a part of that last great crest of the Holy Spirit. All He wants is our *heart* and our *availability*. If we truly want revival, it is time to do something about it! Are you going to be one of those involved in the final move of God's Holy Spirit? Are you going to be one of those involved in destroying the works of the devil in your realm of influence? If you are, then *there is a price to pay.* You are going to have to give God your *heart—all of it!* It is going to take a team of committed Christians who are knitted together in this way, to make the impact that God desires to make in our society today.

NOTES:

[1] Deu. 8:11-20
[2] Deu. 8:1-10
[3] Heb. 12:3-11
[4] Jer. 29:13
[5] John 14:21
[6] Prov. 11:25
[7] John 4:34
[8] Matt. 9:36-38
[9] 1 Tim. 4; 2 Tim. 3; 2 Pet. 2

[10] Haggai 1
[11] Haggai 2
[12] Acts 17:6

15.

PASS OVER JORDAN

"And Moses said unto the people: Remember this day, in which you went out of Egypt, out of the house of bondage; for by strength of hand the Lord brought you out of this place. No leavened bread shall be eaten."

Ex. 13:3

The time is *now!* Shout it from the housetops! The time is come! It is time to Cross over Jordan and to enter into that good land which God has promised us. It is time to enter into that good land which God has given us in the person of the Lord Jesus Christ!

The time *is* now. This one recurrent refrain has echoed throughout our discussions like a resounding chorus—"Cross over the Jordan"! Why, it has even begun to sound like a spiritual battle-cry of sorts.

This brings up an interesting point! Do we truly remember the Jordan? Do we truly remember what those valiant men fought and died for—the courage of their convictions and the circumstances under which they forfeited their lives? Do we remember Moses and Joshua—how they publicly brought Israel to a point of *decision* in their lives?

This decision marked a *turning point* in their life.
Two radically different paths laid there before
them. They could either cross over or they could
choose to remain where they were. The *crossing*
of that line would require a *commitment*. The
crossing *represented* a heart dedication to pursue
what they truly believed in, at all costs! They
fought for all that they held dear. Choosing to risk
their very lives for the mere *promise* of freedom.
They counted the *promise* of freedom and all of its
risks more preferable to the bondage and slavery
of a foreign power. What courage! What conviction!

In Christ Jesus, we possess a far greater
promise of the future.[1] We have a far greater
promise because we *know* what the outcome of
our war is to be. Therefore, we should never lose
hope! We know what the end result of that heroic
sacrifice was—made on the Cross almost 2,000
years ago. Therefore, we should not walk in uncertainty, fear and doubt! We know! If Joshua
and Israel were able to cross that line in the face
of such uncertainty, *how much more* should the
Church of the Lord Jesus Christ make that commitment to Cross the Jordan, *knowing* of that
inheritance which lies before us? How much more
should *we* fight, *knowing* of our future in God's
Kingdom.

Jesus is our Commander-in-Chief. He commands the war that has already been won, a
victory that has already been achieved. He has
commanded us therefore, to take this victory out
into the world.[2]

Jesus is bringing us to a point of decision in our
lives. He has drawn a line in our *hearts*, through
the teaching of the Jordan? We see the Lord

Himself is challenging us to cross that line in our hearts and count the cost, as we cross it. Therefore, we are at a turning point in our lives, just as Joshua and the children of Israel were. Jesus has unleashed the sword of His Word. Which path then, will we take? Which choice will we make? Will we love ourselves more than the promise of God's inheritance? Are we willing to risk all and lose our lives for the Gospel's sake or would we rather hang onto the world and save our lives for our own "self's" sake? Again, the choice is ours but as we consider this choice, Jesus is asking us to remember the Jordan?

As I stated previously, Jesus is drawing a line in our hearts and that line represents the teaching behind the crossing of the Jordan. What we are saying through this battle-cry is that this is the teaching which God wants His Church to take hold of today. We are emphatic in our belief that it is God's express desire for His people to embrace these truths and to walk in them right here and right now! Therefore, we intend to shout it from the housetops. In fact, this is why I have entitled this book, "Who Will Cross The Jordan?"

Remember the Jordan! Remember the Jordan because it should become a spiritual battle-cry in each and every one of our hearts. The Jordan should become a battle-cry within the Church at this particular juncture in its history. Why? Because God recorded the account of the wilderness wanderings strictly for our benefit. 1 Corinthians 10:11 specifically states that these admonitions are for that Church "upon whom the end's of the world are come". That means us! The Church right here and right now! No one has ever been closer to the return of Jesus than we are. Therefore, we need to take careful heed of these admonitions and in taking heed, we need to lift up the standard of the Lord Jesus Christ and march into the land that God has promised us!

Remember the Jordan! Let the cry resound within your hearts. Let's take that first step into the river!

PASS OVER JORDAN
(Written for the 1990 Spiritual Impact/Evangelism Conference)

Pass over Jordan, the waters have been stilled,
The Ark is going forward, His glory is revealed,
Just another footstep, to claim your holy ground,
All that you've been looking for,
The promised land is found!

CHORUS:
Pass over Jordan, Pass over Jordan,
Pass over, leave the past behind,
Will you cross? Will you cross?
Pass over Jordan, the Spirit beckons go,
The waters are receding, your heart shall overflow,
The fullness of Christ in you, the resurrected man,
Once baptized into His death, to rise and live again.

CHORUS: *(Repeat)*

NOTES:

[1] Eph. 1:1-23
[2] Lk. 19:13

164

Turning Point Ministries International

Doug Stringer is the founder and director of Turning Point Ministries International, an evangelistic and discipleship ministry with outreaches to the Church and secular world. The ministry began in 1981 when Doug, a physical fitness instructor and owner of an exercise business, made a decision to totally yield and surrender to the Lordship of Jesus Christ.

Turning Point began very simply in Doug's own exercise studio and apartment. As he began to provide a refuge for the homeless and hurting through physical provision, former drug dealers and addicts, male and female prostitutes, runaways, hitchhikers, even a professional dancer along with members of his dance company, were led to the Real Refuge, a personal relationship with Christ. There were no offices, no minister's licenses and no business cards or decals. There was only the devoted heart of a servant who had confessed, "Lord, whatever it takes, I will serve you."

Through the recognition and encouragement of pastors, ministry leaders and others such as Dr. Edwin Louis Cole, author of *Maximized Manhood, Potential Principle, Courage, Communication Sex and Money*, and others, Doug was inspired to further obedience in his own call. This call led the ministry into organizing, coordinating and involvement with many outreaches such as Jericho Marches (Rock Concert Evangelism), Taking Your City Jericho Drives, Beach Blitz's, Street Feeds, Evangelism through Performing Arts, Spiritual Warfare Meetings, Mardi Gras Outreaches and various other street ministries and outreaches.

Turning Point Ministries has recently changed its name to Turning Point Ministries International because of its outreach into other countries through those discipled and associated with the ministry. Crusades, discipleship training, creative evangelism and mercy missions are just a few ways by which the ministry has reached into areas of the world such as Australia, New Zealand, Europe, Africa, Central America and Asia. Through Doug's frequent travels to Australia, which began by his leading an Australian hitchhiker to the Lord in Houston, Texas, an associate ministry was established named Turning Point Australia. Doug personally has ministered in Australia, Thailand, Vietnam, New Zealand, Central America and others.